...IVERSITY
ORPE CAMPU...

...1400...735

Kennels
and
Kenneling

Kennels *and* Kenneling

A GUIDE FOR PROFESSIONALS AND HOBBYISTS

Joel M. McMains

New York

Maxwell Macmillan Canada
Toronto

Maxwell Macmillan International
New York   Oxford   Singapore   Sydney

Howell Book House
Macmillan Publishing Company
866 Third Avenue
New York, NY 10022

Maxwell Macmillan Canada, Inc.
1200 Eglinton Avenue East
Suite 200
Don Mills, Ontario M3C 3N1

Macmillan Publishing Company is part of the Maxwell Communication Group of Companies.

Library of Congress Cataloging-in-Publication Data

McMains, Joel M.
    Kennels and kenneling / Joel M. McMains.
        p.   cm.
    Includes index.
    ISBN 0-87605-661-3
    1. Kennels.   2. Kennel management.   3. Title.
SF428.M25   1994
636.7′0831—dc20   93-30076
                                                       CIP

Macmillan books are available at special discounts for bulk purchases for sales promotions, premiums, fund-raising, or educational use. For details, contact:

Special Sales Director
Macmillan Publishing Company
866 Third Avenue
New York, NY 10022

10 9 8 7 6 5 4 3 2 1

Printed in the United States of America

In memory of Chattan, my Doberman friend and companion: June 30, 1980–February 8, 1993. He unfailingly made this trainer look good.

Contents

*Until one is committed,
there is hesitancy,
the chance to draw back,
always ineffectiveness.
Concerning all acts of initiative
(and creation) there is
one elementary truth,
the ignorance of which
kills countless ideas
and splendid plans:
That the moment that one
definitely commits oneself,
then Providence moves too.
All sorts of things occur to
help one that would never
otherwise have occurred.
A whole stream of events
issues from the decision,
raising in one's favor all manner
of unforeseen incidents
and meetings and material assistance,
which no man could have dreamed
would come his way.*

W. H. Murray
The Scottish Himalayan Expedition

Acknowledgments

I AM INDEBTED to many good people for their help in the preparation of this book: Ron Flath, Jo Sykes, Roger Davidson, Heather Hodgkins, Sharon Michael, Jim Robinson, Bill and Barb Ziegler, Darryl Dockstader, John Berberick, Richard Moore of Dick's Imagery in Sheridan, Wyoming, for his outstanding photography, Mack Bischoff, DVM, Blair Gustavson, DVM, Denny Peterson, DVM, all of Sheridan, Wyoming, Marilyn Mills of Green Acres Kennels in Rawlins, Wyoming, Seymour Weiss of Howell Book House, who suggested the project, and most of all, H.P. I also thank all the dogs I have ever boarded, for their patience, their wisdom, their love, their lessons, and for their company.

Preface

THIS IS A BOOK about kennels, both as a noun and a verb, transitive and intransitive. While the book's emphasis is on boarding-kennel design and operation, home kennels and breeding and training facilities are also discussed at length. *Kennels and Kenneling*'s boarding section examines plusses and minuses of subjects ranging from design considerations to construction materials to day-to-day operations. The boarding section also offers ideas on advertising, public relations, record keeping, management techniques and business practices in general.

If you are looking for a book that provides definitive, "This is the only way!" answers to each and every question that can arise about kennels, however, your search must continue. To say otherwise is to imply that rock-solid principles applicable to all types of kennels exist, and that is simply not true. Kennel designs and methods of operation are not only direct reflections of purpose, they are as individual and personalized as the owner's fingerprints. A construction or management technique that is successful for one facility might result in disaster for another. There are too many variables attendant to the kennel concept for anyone to claim that any one-size-fits-all method of planning, construction, operation and decision making will be universally effective. Yes, this book offers a wealth of information for everyone from pet owners to hobbyists to professionals, but of equal importance, it provides a direction, helping you to determine questions you need to ask, raising issues you are likely to face and offering possible solutions.

One premise underlying all sections of the book is that the kennel, whatever its purpose, must be more than just adequate, yet it need not rival the Taj Mahal. We are discussing construction and operation of a facility intended for housing and catering to the needs of dogs, not people. The keys are that any kennel must be warm in winter, cool in summer, clean, dry, comfortable, safe and secure always. A second postulate is of three parts. First, that the kennel you envision is a single-story structure not larger than thirty runs; super kennel, mega-run planning is beyond this book's scope, though the management principles offered are applicable for operations of all sizes. Second, the kennel is adjacent to your home; it's on your property. Third, that the kennel operator "knows" *Canis familiaris*; he or she can read a dog, often without conscious effort.

The following thoughts are for those who are considering a career in boarding kennel management. They originally appeared under a subsection entitled "Have You Lost Your Mind?" when I first began this manuscript. The title intended a fleck of humor while making a point: Aspiring boarding kennel operators should do a bit of soul-searching before diving into the business. Running a boarding facility is not the most difficult work in the world, but in addition to being quite time-consuming, it can have negative aspects. Weekend getaways for you are out of the question, being able to count on undisturbed meals or just an evening of visiting with company is a luxury of the past, your phone will ring at strange hours and you won't always be able to get a full night's sleep. Sometimes an uninterrupted cup of coffee will seem a blessing.

In a more serious vein, any dog you board can fall prey to any of a host of illnesses, perhaps endangering other boarders and your own pets. Also, you can find yourself at physical risk from fear-driven or aggressive animals. Customers can cancel reservations at the last minute, or not let you know they have changed their plans at all, and you will occasionally witness permutations of the human-canine relationship that may cause you to have to bite your tongue. The need for maintenance and upkeep is a constant, and—unless you have reliable kennel help—you can forget what a day off is like.

Even given those drawbacks, however, and a good many more, there is nothing that many of us would rather do with our days than take care of and spend time with *Canis familiaris*. A career of managing dogs beats the daylights out of nine-to-five, commuting and office politics. Though boarding-kennel operation is not a growth industry, so long as people own dogs there will be a need for boarding kennels. In many areas of the country, boarding is largely a seasonal business, but not only is it a great way to have continual contact with man's best friend and to have constant opportunities to learn and discover, people are actually willing to pay you to do it.

SECTION I

Home/Breeding/ Training Kennels

1

Home Kennels

THOUGH ANY WORTHWHILE home kennel has elements in common with a boarding facility, there are also significant differences. The most obvious of these is overall size: Few boarding kennels are smaller than five runs, while not many home kennels have more than that number. Also, while both types of facilities must be utilitarian, home kennel owners need not concern themselves about impressing clients with landscaping, structural aesthetics and decor. Their only considerations about a given plan need be, "Will it work?" and "Will my dog be safe and comfortable as a result?" The home kennel owner can prop a piece of faded plywood against a run to provide shade; though that may be a good solution to the problem, the boarding kennel operator who does the same thing risks communicating a bailing-wire-and-chewing-gum atmosphere to clients. He or she operates under the additional concern of, "Will doing this thing cause any of my customers to raise an eyebrow?"

Given the many conceptual similarities between boarding kennels and home kennels, however, I recommend that pet owners contemplating a home facility read both the home kennel and the boarding kennel sections. Some boarding kennel concepts pertaining to design, construction and operation, though obviously not intended for a typical home kennel, may offer ideas that can be modified and adapted to your particular needs.

3

Is This Trip Necessary?

The first question to address in planning a home kennel is "Do I really need one?" Many pet owners have been known to expend significant amounts of money, time and effort constructing a lavish kennel when a secure fence and a well-built doghouse or a dog door leading onto the back porch or basement would have satisfied their needs at far less expense.

An alternative to building a kennel is to upgrade or alter an existing fence pattern. Let's say that you have a large backyard surrounded by a fence that is high enough to contain pooch and deter intruders. You are thinking about building a kennel to centralize your pet's toilet activities. Consider that in this situation it might be wiser from a standpoint of time and expense to merely fence off a small area of your backyard for the purpose. Then, each time that it is obvious that the animal has done in the fenced-off area what he needed to do, the dog could be released into the larger yard for exercise purposes. True, the dog may still occasionally mark certain areas of your backyard—dogs do that sort of thing, you know—but the bulk of the leavings will be in one relatively small area, making for much easier cleanups.

Please understand, I would never foster a "get-by" attitude when it comes to caring for man's best friend. Our pets are important to us, and their housing should be more than just okay. At the same time, I would do you a disservice not to suggest that you begin by first asking, "Is a kennel 'right' for my situation?"

Codes, Covenants and Zoning

Before looking up the current price of chain-link fencing (be seated when you do that, by the way), ascertain that your planned kennel will not violate any local building codes, covenants, ordinances or zoning regulations. It is no good to invest in building any structure only to have to try to placate unhappy neighbors and chronic complainers after the fact.

Rule of Design #1

In planning your kennel the primary consideration should be your pet's security and comfort, not "Where can I make this thing fit?" If the site you plan would have pooch next to your property line, thereby exposing the dog to possible teasing or worse, or would provide inadequate shade from summer sun or meager shelter from winter harshness, rethink.

Other Design Considerations

Is your proposed location close to a water source? If not, you will have to either extend a water line to the kennel area or resign yourself to carrying water daily (at least) to the animal. You will also have to extend hoses for cleaning purposes. Considerations such as these come under the heading of future efficiency. Carrying a bucket of water to pooch or dragging a hose to the kennels may seem to be trivial matters, but remember that they are tasks you will have to perform every day for several years. Further, should you later acquire additional dogs, you will be carrying additional buckets.

A related consideration is the location of your kennel relative to existing electric sources and sewer lines (assuming you envision using electricity at your kennel site, or tapping into sewer lines). Locating a kennel near electricity sources makes for much easier installation of outside lighting, which is an important security consideration. The desirability of sewer accessibility is obvious, though you should be sure that making access into a local system is legal.

A second reason for situating your kennel close to electric sources relates to the possibility of change in your personal circumstances. Perhaps you will someday find that you are having to leave your dogs more than you thought you would. Nearby power can make for much easier installation of water-bucket heaters, self-feeders and other conveniences.

Another point to ponder is that of combining projects. If you have been thinking about building a workshop, for example, or a storage shed or a similar out-building, perhaps you could make the kennel part of your proposed building.

Consider your neighbors, too. If one of two otherwise equal locations would make for quieter housing in terms of people who live nearby, choose that site. Also, be aware that placement of your kennel can affect your property values: A well-located kennel can raise them, though one that is poorly situated can have the opposite effect.

Overall Size

A revered trainer who has forgotten more about kennel design and operation than many of us have ever known once gave me a piece of advice about run construction that has proven accurate numerous times: ''Figure out how many runs you think you need, double that number, then build that many runs.'' The point my friend was making was that dog owners often increase their number of dogs, and that it is generally easier and less expensive to erect four runs at one time, for instance, than it is to build two now and try to add two more later. A basic application of the rationale underlying this thinking concerns the individual who owns a dog, builds a run and then—through perhaps unforeseen circumstances—acquires a puppy. The older animal likes the pup but sometimes wants to play too rough, and the owner now has a problem of what to do with one of his pets while he cannot be present.

While it is important not to underbuild, of equal or even greater importance is the notion of allowing in your original plans the possibility of subsequent expansion. More than one pet owner has evolved into a hobbyist and then into at least a semi-professional in some area of canine-related activities. Perhaps such a metamorphic process will never happen to you, but always leave yourself room to grow nonetheless.

Run Size

Though boarding kennel runs are traditionally between three and five feet wide and are of varying lengths, for a home kennel run to be both useful and comfortable for your dog, it must provide room for exercise; the pooch should be able to take at least a few quick steps. Remember, the structures are called ''runs,'' not ''shuffles.''

Though the amount of room available at your building site may make the decision for you, at least up to a point, you may want to size your runs as though you owned large dogs, even if your pets are small ones. Flexibility is the key here, because later expansion of the size of existing runs is even more difficult than is adding new ones. True, Scotties may be the only breed in the world for you; but that's today, and absolutes have a way of changing. One woman who started out with Beagles used to tell me, ''There's no dog like them!'' (which is true of any breed, of course). Today she has one aged Beagle and three young Chesapeake Bay Retrievers (she tells me there is no breed like Chessies, either). The old cliché that cautions against painting oneself into a corner is applicable here.

Besides, someday you may move. Sheltie-sized runs might seem more of a liability than an asset to a prospective buyer who owns Golden Retrievers. That person's reaction might be, ''I'll have to rip

6

those runs out and start over,'' which, of course, would entail more work and expense than would be necessitated by starting from scratch, and could lead a prospective buyer to look elsewhere.

Run Surface

Concrete, gravel and dirt are the common options. Boarding kennels often choose concrete simply because it is the easiest surface to clean generally and to disinfect specifically. However, concrete is also the most expensive choice, and though a boarding kennel has to disinfect runs quite often, do you feel that you need to sanitize your pet's quarters several times daily against every germ known to dog-dom? Your pooch is going to be the only dog in the kennel, and it's pretty hard for a healthy animal to catch a disease from itself, you know. Yes, any kennel should be *periodically* debugged, but does that mean that you need to go to the expense and effort of concrete simply to facilitate an infrequent task?

Consider, too, that concrete can be as much of a risk to a canine's well-being as can many diseases. Boarders seldom show the wearing effects of being on the unyielding surface because they are housed at boarding kennels for relatively short periods. A dog on concrete for many hours a week, though, year in and year out, will develop elbow calluses at least and skeletal problems at worst. Notice how your feet and legs feel after continually standing on the hard surface for just a few hours, even when you are wearing well-constructed, comfortable shoes. Prolonged confinement on concrete eventually breaks down any animal.

But, can gravel or dirt be disinfected? Up to a point, yes. Using a scrub brush and squeegee is out of the question, of course, which means that more disinfecting solution has to be used as it literally has to be poured over the area to saturate it (and hosed into the earth afterward), but again: How often does one need to disinfect a run that is occupied always and only by the same dog? Remember, too, that one of nature's best germ killers, sunlight, can zap many surface microbes. Disinfecting, per se, is intended for nooks and crannies where sunlight cannot effectively reach and to get the bugs that the sun's ultraviolet rays, and the resulting drying action, does not exterminate.

Another consideration is that gravel is easier to install than concrete. Fewer tools are required—a wheelbarrow and a shovel make up the list—and the job seldom necessitates contracting skilled labor, which likely would be needed for pouring and finishing concrete. Being less permanent than concrete, gravel is vulnerable to digging, but gravel's impermanence can also be a positive attribute should one ever wish to eliminate the kennel structure. Granted, removing packed gravel is a job, but taking out concrete can make a person wish that he or she had never heard of the substance. Other than the occasional determined (if ill-advised) weed that makes it through the stones, gravel offers home kennel builders a sound, practical alternative to concrete, if for no other reason than it is much less wearing on a dog than confinement on concrete.

Of course, were the dogs themselves allowed a vote they would likely opt for dirt-surfaced runs. Dirt is natural, more comfortable than any hard surface, and of utmost importance (to a dog, at least), it is a digger's dream come true. The only real drawback to dirt runs from an owner's point of view, other than it is easy to dig, is that dirt naturally makes for dirty dogs, especially during wet weather. That's when dirt quickly becomes mud and, covered with the stuff, an adorable pet quickly becomes an adorable mudball. One cringes at the thought of pooch trotting across the living room carpet, or shaking itself near the sofa. The animal must be bathed and dried before being brought into the house's living area, and by the time some of the long-haired breeds are sufficiently dry to allow them run of the house, it's time to put them out for a walk again. Dirt runs may be okay for outdoor dogs (or in arid locales), but gravel or concrete is preferable for house pets.

If you elect to go with either dirt- or gravel-surfaced runs, bury rust-resistant, wire-mesh fencing three inches below the run's surface; lay the fencing material flat, at a right angle to the run's sides. The purpose, of course, is to prevent pooch from tunneling under the run panels.

Should you decide that concrete is your preference, make the pad at least four inches thick and slope it away from the dog's rest area to promote runoff of liquids. Depending on the pad's overall size, you may want to reinforce it with wire mesh, but that—along with determining the pad's thickness—gets into an area where you should seek the opinion of a professional mason.

Run Fencing Materials

Though boarding kennel operators generally prefer chain-link enclosure panels and gates, pet owners can be more flexible in their planning. True, chain-link fencing is well suited to run construction, but it is also very expensive and often necessitates hiring skilled labor for installation. If one keeps a few basics in mind, however, serviceable runs can be erected with comparative ease and far less cost using non-climb fencing and wooden posts.

Non-climb fencing is readily available at many lumberyards and hardware stores. The material, which comes in a variety of heights, is durable, comparatively inexpensive and relatively easy to install.

When shopping for wooden posts, make sure to select those that have been treated against insects and moisture so as not to have to replace them in years to come because of infestation or rot. Though it may not be absolutely necessary, setting the posts in concrete makes for a more solid structure than does tamping them in with dirt. You may not wish to set all posts in concrete, but I do recommend that you set at least the corner posts and gateposts in concrete for stability and longevity.

Tools needed for non-climb fencing and wooden-post construction are a shovel, a post-hole digger, a tamping bar, a fence stretcher (also known as a come-along), boards for clamping the fencing for stretching, a heavy chain for wrapping around the boards and attaching to the fence stretcher, a level, a fencing tool (your hardware dealer will know what this item is), a wheelbarrow and a hammer. As some of these items are expensive, you may want to consider renting certain ones rather than making outright purchases.

Depending on the character of area soil and related factors (sand and gravel content, ground-water level and so forth), set at least 25 percent of each post's length into the ground (check with local builders and suppliers for specific recommendations). Wherever possible, configure your runs so that the fencing will be attached between the posts and pooch to lessen the opportunity for chewing. If you elect to cover the tops of the runs with fencing, which is a sound security precaution, make the runs tall enough so that you can stand in them without having to stoop. Also, in planning run height, remember that packed snow on a run's surface can quickly reduce the run fencing's effective height.

Other Run Considerations

While boarding-kennel runs are generally erected with permanence in mind, pet owners are not bound by any such principle. Unhampered by concerns about pleasing anyone other than yourself and your dog, you have options in areas of design and construction where a boarding kennel operator would feel constrained by restrictions born of convention. Of course, your runs should be secure in the sense that no common force should be able to topple them, but that does not imply that they must be installed in a nondetachable manner. Many retail, mass-merchandiser catalogs, as well as those of businesses offering canine specialty products, offer bolt-together chain-link panels that might be perfect not just for renters, but for people who would like to have the option of taking the structure with them should they move.

Another point to ponder is that pet-kennel owners do not *have* to build using new equipment. Boarding-kennel people often are left with little choice, as much of their chain-link fencing is custom-designed and made-to-order. When constructing my boarding kennel, however, had I been able to locate used chain-link fencing and gates of certain dimensions and degrees of slope (as well as a few other little niceties), I would have been sorely tempted to grab the used equipment as I likely could have saved a bundle. Before you spring for new materials, peruse the classified sections of local newspapers and shopper's guides for used fencing; also check local radio stations' for-sale-or-trade programs. As I've suggested more than once in this chapter, chain-link is expensive stuff, and while new and shiny is always nice, it's not always *that* nice.

Waste Disposal

Though the number of one's pets can figure in the decision of how best to keep runs clean (as can public-health rules in some regions), for most home kennel owners a scoop designed for the purpose and a garbage can double-lined with heavy-duty trash sacks—along with taking pains to stay on good terms with the trash collectors—are often the most economical ways of removing solid wastes. Concrete-surfaced runs emptying into a sloped trough perpendicular to and beyond the run's length is common in boarding kennel construction, but unless you have several dogs and wish to go to the expense of installing a septic system into which the trough can empty, such a setup—though unarguably efficient and easy to use—represents needless additional costs, which can be considerable. Surrounding the run pad with a bed of gravel several inches deep, into which urine and cleaning solutions can be hosed and drained away, is generally adequate for most home kennel setups.

Security

This section addresses prevention against escape or intrusion. I have already mentioned the notions of burying wire mesh under gravel- or dirt-surfaced runs, and installing fencing atop the runs. The purpose behind both tasks is to protect a dog from its own impulses (i.e., digging or climbing out). A strong padlock takes care of the run gate, and a secure fence around the area completes the picture by making escape or unlawful entry doubly difficult. Granted, a fenced yard in addition to a kennel may seem superfluous, but in addition to increased security, it offers many options and advantages. Exercise, convenience (you won't have to put a leash on pooch to transport to or from the kennel) and nonconfinement in the kennel as the only way of having your pet outside are just a few.

If it happens that you have no choice but to put your kennel along a property fence, which is not desirable but is sometimes inevitable, make the side of the run that abuts the fence solid and impenetrable. This makes fence fighting with neighboring dogs unlikely, and it may also inhibit children from teasing your pet. Were a child to put a hand through a fence into your dog's run and be injured, you could wind up facing a lawsuit.

Housing

The most common forms of canine housing are a doghouse or attaching the run to a house or a heated garage and installing an access door. As those solutions usually are also the most practical, this section concentrates upon those two areas.

If you decide to go the doghouse route, consider two basic options: placing the structure within the run, or placing it outside the run and attaching the run to it. Placing the doghouse in the run itself offers more security as the animal is always behind a gate that can be locked. At the same time, with runs lacking fencing across their tops, lessened security can be the result if the dog is of such a size as to be able to climb atop the doghouse to take a shot at going over the top of the run. Also, placing a wooden doghouse inside a run can promote chewing, a canine option that is lessened by situating the house outside the fence and attaching the run to it. Whatever you decide about placement, be aware that heated doghouses as well as heated floor surfaces are on the market. Such products can be extremely valuable to those of us not living in the tropics. However, there is one style of doghouse to avoid: those made of metal. They can prove to be next to useless and even hazardous during times of extreme heat or cold.

Though prefabricated doghouses are available in various materials from numerous sources, you may wish to build one yourself. Regarding doghouse layout and construction, consider the following general floor plan.

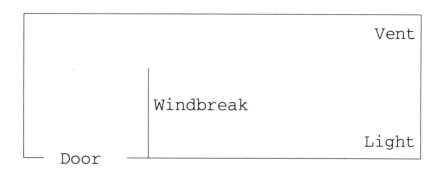

The *door* should face away from prevailing winds. The *windbreak*, which can be made of plywood and should extend from floor to ceiling, reaches slightly more than halfway across the house's depth. Its purpose is to create a secure, dry, wind-free area for your pet. Chewing can be discouraged by attaching heavy metal sheathing to the windbreak's exposed edge, as well as to those of the doorway. *Light* refers to a bulb of minimal but adequate wattage to provide heat; it should be installed in an unbreakable, waterproof (and dog-proof) fixture near the ceiling. All wiring should be shielded in metal conduit. The *vent*, which should also be installed near the ceiling, should be of a louvered design that repels moisture while promoting drying.

The entire structure—walls, ceiling and floor—should be insulated and should be raised slightly above the ground to promote drying and avoid floor rotting. In elevating the house, take care to situate it in a manner that will not allow pooch to move or tip it. The overall design should allow for only slightly more space than the dog is large. Humans tend to transfer their own needs and wants into the making of a doghouse by building too large and roomy a structure. However, because dogs like small, tight, secure nests, a doghouse that is too large won't get used. Pooch should be able to turn around inside the doghouse, but he needs no more room than that.

The roof should be sloped to promote water runoff, but make this angle slight if the house is inside the run (or behind a secure fence) so the dog can climb atop it to sun himself, as most dogs love to do. Finally, one can optionally hinge the roof (or make it detachable) to facilitate cleaning.

For comfort's sake, you may wish to cover the floor by installing a wall-to-wall section of indoor-outdoor carpeting. Surround the carpeting with quarter-section wood molding to discourage your pet from chewing on an edge. Don't just put cloth scraps in the doghouse; attach them. Otherwise, whatever you put in will be dragged out.

If you have a heated garage, using a portion of it (or of your house) instead of a doghouse for your pet's nest can marginally affect overall cost. Though the need for a doghouse may be eliminated, an interior pen will likely be required to confine your pet to one area. Attaching runs to a heated garage (or house, or a heated out-building) can be a sound move provided there is no possibility that your dog can escape into the garage or house, perhaps wreaking havoc on the contents and/or injuring itself. For security reasons, and for times when you want to confine pooch to either an inside or outside run, you should be able to lock the door to the outside-run area. Also, keep four cautions in mind. First, make both the inside and the outside enclosures four-sided, not three-sided. True, the wall of the building provides a fourth side for both; it can also provide too much temptation for a chewer, especially when a bored animal is confined in proximity to such tempting material. Second, realize that the building must have adequate interior drains to allow for disposal of cleaning solutions. Third, if you are using part of your garage for your pet's nest, make certain that the building is very well ventilated: Carbon monoxide and other vehicular emissions do not play favorites—they only kill. Fourth, consider that in the tragic event of fire, pooch may be unable to flee far enough from the blaze to avoid injury or death.

Care and Comfort

Providing your pet with something safe to chew can greatly relieve boredom. A nearby radio playing gentle if not droning music can be soothing to a lonely dog. Avoid hard rock or intense debate programming, however, as such noise can create anxiety. Blankets can afford a comfortable nesting area, but take them away from pooch if there is a tendency to chew them: Ingestion of cloth or similar materials can be fatal. Avoid the use of straw and the like, which can make for an insect haven as well as a fire hazard. Constant access to cool, clean water is a necessity, of course, but neither the dog's food nor water should be placed where they can be affected by anyone other than family members. As you know, our aptly named criminal-justice system does a more than adequate job of ensuring that a number of degenerate minds are continually loose on society. Dogs can also be victims.

A closing thought for this subsection concerns the concept of a first-aid kit for your pet. If you don't have one, get one. If you do have one, keep it in a constant location known to all adult family members.

The contents of a complete kit (which you may wish to modify—your vet can tell you what you need to have on hand) is outlined in chapter 5, "Equipment and Supplies." Also, a first-aid reference chart appears at the end of this book.

The Taxman Cometh

A seemingly minor point that can later prove crucial is the fact that—like any addition to your house—you should keep careful records pertaining to the cost of your kennel. Should you ever sell your property, the receipts and such that relate to the kennel's construction could be quite useful when computing taxes.

Lest Ye Forget

There is a subtle effect that the availability of a kennel can have on the relationship between dog and owner, especially in the case of house pets.

The kennel is finished, all is in readiness and pooch is placed therein, "To try it out, you know." But over time the animal comes to spend progressively more hours in the enclosure, though not by choice. Kenneling, perhaps originally envisioned by the owner for use only for toilet purposes and when the family is away, develops into a habit. Banishment becomes routine, occasioned by such noteworthy events as company stopping by, or watching the big game, or the little game, or because it is Tuesday. Though the dog would much rather be with what used to be family, such closeness soon becomes a fading series of memories. The dog begins to find a hole in its life where people used to be.

I bring this to your attention only because I have witnessed the phenomenon and its subtle, insidious growth and distancing effect too many times. In my book *Advanced Obedience Training—Easier Than You Think!*, I caution against a dangerous tendency to which some people can become prey: "Don't fall into the trap of allowing yourself to become so engrossed in training and competition that you forget why you ever got a dog in the first place." Excessive kenneling can foster an even riskier malignancy, because then the separation is physical as well as spiritual. By definition a kennel is a place for a dog, yes, but from the view that pooch is your best buddy, a healthier definition is that a kennel is an *occasional* place for a dog. Water-bucket heaters and self-feeders are all very nice, though sometimes such gadgets

14

contribute to making it easier to care for an animal's needs through automation rather than through contact, and to keeping pooch from family. Consider, too, with regard to the concept of water-bucket heaters, for example, if the temperature is such that water in a large container can freeze, though a heater may circumvent the problem, the message may be that the dog should be brought in to share the warmth of the home. Excessive kenneling is jail time, nothing less, for crimes uncommitted.

Reflection

The method of the enterprising is to plan with audacity, and execute with vigor; to sketch out a map of possibilities, and then to treat them as probabilities.

Christian Nelson Bovee

2

Of Interest to Breeders and Trainers

BREEDERS

Though *Kennels and Kenneling* is a not represented as a breed book, it offers suggestions to help breeders establish a kennel or upgrade an existing one, as well as ideas about dam and puppy maintenance and welfare. With those thoughts in mind, breeders should read the Kennel Name and Advertising and Public Relations parts of chapter 4, "Startup," as well as the following chapters:

1. "Home Kennels"
3. "Planning, Design and Construction" (*Boarding Kennels* section)
5. "Equipment and Supplies" (*Boarding Kennels* section)

With the exception of whelping facilities and a few general guidelines, discussions of which follow shortly, those recommended sections of the book contain material that are relevant to establishing a breeding kennel. This is because many breeding kennels are a combination of a home kennel and a boarding facility; they are generally somewhere in between, in terms of the physical plant. The primary difference is one of objective: puppy production, rather than a place to house other people's dogs.

Maternity Ward Appointments

In addition to a kennel facility for housing young and mature dogs, breeders need a whelping area. More to the point, their bitches need one. Sure, many a healthy litter has been produced on the floor of the guest-bedroom closet, but a professional breeder should have more professional facilities.

Removed from all noise and confusion—that's the first rule about how to site a whelping area. Just as the guest-bedroom closet is not the perfect place, neither is an unoccupied run in a kennel building. In fact, the ideal whelping site is not located anywhere in or even near a kennel—the risk of disease transmission from other animals to the dam and her pups is just too great. The best location for a whelping area is an area in your home where you can control access and where day-to-day traffic is at a minimum. No, the dam should not be isolated from her family—the idea is certainly not to ostracize her; it's to give her a secure, peaceful, special place. Barking dogs, ringing phones and doorbells, the presence of strangers, and children running through the area at full yell do not make for a desirable whelping area. Such noises are not merely distracting, they are disturbing, unsettling and can even be seen by a dam as threatening. Some very powerful drives (instincts) are going to be in full operation during the next few days and weeks, and while no canine ever needs a nerve-wracking, seemingly hostile environment, a dam needs one even less.

The whelping area should be dry, well ventilated, easily cleaned, and you should be able to regulate its temperature as precisely as you can that of your home. It should be small enough that the dam can feel secure—too large an area can seem unsafe to a canine, as though there is too much room to defend, while too small an area can seem cramped and stifling. The whelping room should have soft, clean bedding, and cool, fresh water should be available at all times. Keep a supply of paper towels on hand, as well as sanitized kitchen gloves (sterilized surgical gloves are even better), and various first-aid supplies (a complete list of health items appears in chapter 5, "Equipment and Supplies"). Also, there should be a book dealing with emergency veterinary procedures that pertain to whelping, and the breeder should be thoroughly familiar with its contents.

Those are musts. Niceties include an intercom so you can monitor activities in the whelping area without having to be there—many dams like uninterrupted periods of solitude—perhaps a radio tuned to a soft-music station, pen and paper for noting noteworthy events and a portable telephone for contacting your vet (if needed) without having to leave the dam to do so.

Maternity Ward Management

The foregoing covers the physical aspects of a professional whelping area; now consider management issues. The dam should be taken to the site for short periods once you have determined that she is indeed carrying a litter. The purpose of such visits, of course, is familiarization. Ten minutes before the first pup is born is not the time to introduce the dam to the whelping area. A few days before the blessed event is due, move the dam into the whelping area for the duration. Still allow her to take periodic walks outside—she will tell you when—but make the whelping site her temporary home.

A Peanut Gallery?

I have been asked more than once for my opinion on allowing children to be present as puppies are born. It is difficult to formulate a blanket rule for this option as every child is an individual. Like their adult counterparts, some have enough sense to deal with such an important moment properly, some others do not. But since my primary concern during whelping is the dam and her litter, I tend to counsel that it is usually best for her sake to have but one or two adults present in whom the dam has confidence, period. When a perceptive listener has commented that my reply seemed to sidestep the question about allowing children to be present, I have been known to observe that it seems to me an inconsistency to infuse immaturity into a mature situation. The kids will have enough fun playing with the puppies in the weeks to come—as well they should: Children and puppies are made for each other. In the meantime, allow the dam an atmosphere of serenity and confidence. She deserves nothing less.

A Little Consideration, Please

An experienced breeder can spot a "lesser than" puppy soon after birth. An experienced breeder also knows that if any or all of a litter proves disappointing, such thoughts are best kept to oneself; they are not expressed around the dam. It is not that she would necessarily understand your words, but she is familiar with your tones. That animal knows you pretty well, and she senses when you are less than pleased.

19

She has done her job to the best of her ability, now the breeder must do likewise by telling her how beautiful each puppy is, regardless of the truth of the situation.

Soapboxing

One of the perks attendant to writing books is that you can express an opinion now and then that has absolutely nothing to do with the overall subject matter but everything to do with a more encompassing concern. (Of course, you have to hope that your editor will not redline the section, but that is part of the game.)

First, consider that properly designed kennels, comfortable whelping areas and custom-printed pedigrees are all very well, but for the sake of those puppies (and of dogs generally), please: Do not breed unless you are absolutely certain that you will be able to find homes for each puppy, and make that *good* homes. The number of unwanted dogs destroyed annually at local shelters is disgraceful. If you are planning a litter, and if you know that a typical litter for your breed is X number of puppies, get *at least* that many responsible owners lined up prior to breeding. If you cannot find that many people now, what makes you think that you can do so once the pups are on the ground? I offer this advice to all breeders, but especially to those who own some of the rarer, more exotic breeds, as those puppies can be more difficult to place.

Point two: I mentioned *good* homes. As defining such a home— a family, really—is difficult in terms of matching prospective buyers to a list of desirable attributes, it is one of those situations where you go with what your gut tells you, and follow the rule of "If in doubt, pass." Never let a pup go to a home you do not feel good about. Elements such as a nice house in a good part of town, steady employment, regular churchgoers, 2.3 children and so on are interesting statistics but they reveal absolutely nothing about character, compassion and a healthy sense of self-worth. When I visit with a prospective owner, it is for longer than just a few minutes; and though mine may seem a reverse approach, I consciously look for reasons *not* to place a pup with the individual, not for reasons *to* place a pup. Reasons *to* will make themselves evident; reasons *not* to will be less apparent—they will be masked by the person—which is why I look for their existence in the first place.

One other gauge I rely upon concerns my own adult dogs. As they are friendly, outgoing animals, if they do not feel good about an individual, then that person does not get one of my pups, pure and simple. I have been told that this is overdoing it, but each pup unknowingly trusts me to make the right choice, and since they are my pups I can do—or not do—anything I want for them without having to justify my decision or how I arrived at it. You have the same responsibility and the same freedom.

End of sermon.

Paperwork and Transfer Practices

As there are procedures a boarding kennel operator follows when releasing a pet to a client, so there should be practices pertaining to transferring a puppy to a new owner. The first is a bill of sale that describes the pup as to (AKC or similar) litter registration number, breed, gender, color, markings and the names and ages (and AKC or similar registration numbers, if applicable) of the sire and dam. The document should also include the whelping date and location, the breeder's name and address, date of sale and the purchase price. AKC or similar registration forms, a record of vaccinations the puppy has received and the dates when the next shots are due should also be given to the buyer along with a multi-generation pedigree. A few-days' supply of whatever food to which the puppy is accustomed, and copies of any puppy photographs you may have taken and pictures of the parents are thoughtful touches. Buyers should also be given a copy of whatever contractual agreement you may have reached, copies of temperament-testing records you may have used and a list of local veterinarians (if the buyer is from your locale).

The actual transfer of the puppy should be accomplished over a period of an hour or so. Start the separation process by bringing the little one to an area that is well away from the litter. Encourage (through insistence, if need be) the buyer to spend some "get-acquainted" time with the pup before departing. For a puppy to leave the only home he has ever known is stressful, obviously, and a two-minute "Here's your pup—good-bye" transfer process greatly heightens that unrest. A gentle, gradual handing-over is not only much easier on the pup, it gives you a chance to get a final reading on the buyer. Have I ever called off a sale at this stage? No, but only because I have never felt that I needed to.

I also furnish buyers with a copy of *Having to Do with Puppies*, a general how-to booklet on puppy raising and management that I wrote some years ago. It is reprinted below, and though copy-machine

HAVING TO DO WITH PUPPIES

Feeding

Puppies attain 80 percent of their eventual growth within six to twelve months. In the process, they burn nearly double the daily calories, pound for pound, that mature dogs do.

From weaning (which is generally around four weeks) until a year, litters should be fed the best puppy-kibble (dry food) that can be had. Price should not be a consideration. When this solid food is first given, stir in water to facilitate mastication and ingestion. Gradually phase out this liquefying practice so that by seven or eight weeks of age, the young ones' nourishment is presented to them completely dry.

Feed the pups four times daily from the time of weaning until they are ten to twelve weeks old, when the night feeding should be eliminated. At five months, switch to morning and evening meals. This change establishes the feeding pattern to follow throughout adult life. At about a year, switch to a maintenance-grade kibble during the warm months, and to one slightly higher in fat and protein content for the cold seasons.

While I would never remove a dog's food bowl while the animal is in mid-bite, nonetheless I allow my pets only ten minutes or so to consume a meal. Then the food dishes are removed, washed and put away until the next scheduled feeding. Dogs are naturally fast eaters, hence the existence of such expressions as, "Dogs wolf their food." The main reason for this canine tendency of eating quickly is that in the wild, a canine's natural setting, one eats as fast as possible, lest other animals covet the meal or circumstances cause its abandonment.

Avoid the practice of "on-demand" feeding, whereby food is available at all times. The procedure can cause boredom, finicky eating habits and obesity. Of equal importance, it eliminates from the animal's emotional menu the possibility for intimate daily contacts between dog and human, the essence of which has as much to do with positive bonding as with proper nutrition. Scheduled meals also afford the advantage of letting you know right away if your pet should go off his feed, which can often represent the first sign of numerous physical and emotional disorders.

Snacks and Such

As far as when tidbits are appropriate—and when they are not—consider this example. When calling puppy into the house, present a biscuit once the dog arrives indoors. Rather than make this a constant practice, reward about three times out of four. That way, curiosity whether there will be a tidbit can operate and draw him or her to you. If a puppy learns that a biscuit will always be offered, the little one may begin to take the practice for granted.

However, do not use food to bribe. That is, in calling puppy to the house, do not stand by the door and wave the treat as you call the pooch. Otherwise, you are offering the pup a choice whether to come, which is not a good idea at any age: Pooch could decide that he would rather persist at whatever he is doing than stop for a snack just then. Get the dog inside, then present the morsel.

You may feed certain table scraps in small amounts (but not chicken bones and the like, which can be harmful—even deadly) as part of scheduled feedings. Permissible between-meal snacks are dog biscuits, which should be given in moderation.

Cool, Clear Water

Dogs of any age should have fresh water available during waking hours. Providing it in galvanized pails ensures they receive a daily trace of zinc, often unavailable in commercial foods. Zinc is an important nutritional element to canines, especially to breeds with erect to semierect ears, as the chemical is thought to contribute to strong ear stance.

Teething

A puppy begins to cut permanent teeth around sixteen weeks. Ease this uncomfortable time by providing rawhide chews, Nylabones and the like. Gently massaging the young one's gums not only alleviates discomfort, it further strengthens the bond forming between you.

Housing and Housebreaking

A new puppy should sleep at bedside in a properly sized, individual airline cage. This practice can eliminate much grief from housebreaking because a sound animal will not consistently foul his sleeping area, provided that he is allowed ample opportunity to seek relief at suitable locations. At bedtime, afford puppy a final evening walk, then take him straightaway to the cage.

While first placing the pup in the enclosure, repeat the word "Nest" several times. The word best expresses the idea to communicate to the little one. The weekend is often an opportune time to acquaint puppy with the nest, as some sleep may be lost that first night, by both of you. To lessen undue worry and whining, place in the cage ahead of time such puppy treasures as a soft towel, maybe a ticking clock, possibly a Nylabone, or perhaps an undershirt you wore that day (probably for the last time). Do not let a dog—young or old—shred a cloth article, however, as ingestion of such material can be fatal.

A pup finding himself alone in such a new situation may whine and fuss a bit, but after a time will usually settle. If the young one becomes unreasonably vocal, and if you are certain that the dog is not telling you that he *must* get outside (or is frightened), a squirt from a spray bottle filled with cold water can do wonders. Accompany such disciplinary measures with a curt (but not roared) "Out!" meaning, "Not now," or more specifically in this case, "Hush." As the puppy calms, praise "Good Out."

Avoid moving the nest about the house. Part of its function is to create a sense of order and stability in and for a puppy. Periodic cage relocation can defeat this purpose. Similarly, other pets or children should not be permitted to enter or play with a pup's cage. The enclosure is something the young canine needs to think of as his, and his nose will tell him if there have been visitors.

The very first thing in the morning, take the puppy outdoors, repeating the cue "Yard" as you transport him there. If the nest is some distance from the door, prevent undesirable stops along the way by carrying the pup. Once the animal is back inside, keep your attention on the dog and be ready to take him outside hurriedly. Should you be occupied with some activity for a time—even just talking on the phone—put the puppy in his nest before proceeding.

Bear in mind that puppies initially possess very little internal control. An active pup involved in play and such would rather continue with what he is doing than stop to expel toxins. Thus, nature has constructed him in such a way that until he gains some maturity, he is simply unable to hold back the dam for more than a few seconds after his little brain issues the word. Once your pup gets "that look" in his eyes, you have very little time to get him outside.

24

The first time the puppy does goof in the house—and most pups do at least once—point his nose close to (but not into) the site of the transgression and repeat the word "No," in a firm, drawn-out manner. Do not speak harshly as that could frighten. More than one overly vocal owner has taught his pet through displays of righteous anger that the animal's natural urges were wrong. "Not here" is the message to communicate, not shame.

After drawing attention to the problem area, tote the puppy outside, encouragingly saying the word "Yard," as you proceed. Gathering up the accident and placing it at the location you want frequented can be helpful. The pup will find and sniff it, and will soon begin to get the idea.

As the young one performs his functions outside, praise (but softly, so as not to distract), saying, "Good piddle, good dump," or whatever phraseology you prefer. Later, during lengthy drives, telling your pet at a rest stop to "Go piddle" will often trigger the desired response.

During puppy's waking hours, regardless of whether he sends signals, make sure to take him outside every couple of hours. Also, walk him after naps, meals and prolonged drinking; those are times when puppies often feel the need.

Unless you have no choice, avoid using newspapers for relief areas. "Paper training" is just that—it can teach a dog to respond to the feel of paper underfoot. Not only can a pup not tell the difference between today's paper and the one you intend for him to use, but more importantly he is being taught to use your house as a bathroom. True, the animal is standing on a newspaper, but that does not change the fact that elimination is occurring in your living space.

Exercise and Socialization

Proper exercise is as important to the well-being of a puppy as is proper nutrition. Without either, healthy physiological or psychological development cannot occur. Your pet needs plenty of play area and lots of playtime with you.

Socialization entails taking a new puppy with you, wherever and whenever circumstances permit. During life's first months, the number and quality of different situations, people and events a pup experiences can affect him for the rest of his days. Always keeping him on-leash, take your young dog to public parks, school areas or just for a drive. If you intend for your pet to be a member of your pack (family), treat him like one.

When taking a dog (young or mature) for outings, *never* leave him unattended in a vehicle. The result can be chewed seats, a stolen pet or heatstroke. This last, which is often fatal, can quickly occur with outside temperatures no warmer than 70 degrees.

Veterinarians

Like your family physician, your vet should be someone in whom you have confidence. (For information about locating a veterinarian, peruse the subsection Vet Shopping in chapter 7, "Policies, Practices and Direction.") As a precautionary measure, any new puppy should be examined before or very soon after arriving at his new home.

Worms and Other Internal Parasites

Periodically take fecal samples to your vet for examination. If the tests are positive, treat the condition according to his or her instructions. Ask your DVM about heartworm preventive and the testing that must precede its initial use.

Shots and Vaccinations

After concluding puppy shots, your pet should be vaccinated yearly against Distemper, Leptospirosis, Hepatitis, Parvo, Rabies, Corona and Tracheobronchitis (Kennel Cough). The vaccination for Tracheobronchitis is comparatively new. If the vet is unwilling to order it for you, find another doctor. A concerned professional realizes that your pet's health comes first.

Medications

Giving pills and liquids are simple tasks that are made easier by conditioning during puppyhood. Give the pups placebos occasionally, always following such treatments with much praise and a biscuit. The treat not only lends a positive accent to the event, it makes sure the medication went down.

To give a pill, open the dog's mouth by reaching over the muzzle and inserting a fingertip directly behind a canine tooth. This causes nearly any dog to open its mouth. Holding the animal's nose upward, quickly but smoothly push the pill toward the back of the tongue.

Withdraw your hand and gently hold the muzzle closed while softly stroking downward along the front of the throat.

To administer a liquid, first draw the fluid into a syringe. Then remove the needle and place the instrument's tip (repeat: *without* a needle attached) in the fold of your pet's cheek near the back teeth while using minimal pressure to hold the muzzle barely closed. Don't plunge the liquid in so quickly that your dog inhales the substance rather than swallows it.

Grooming

Canines usually shed two or three times a year. Gently brush your pup twice a week. Bathe him as needed but not more than six times yearly, lest you dry the skin and coat. Trim nails and clean ears at least weekly. Since there are breed differences as to how these chores are best performed, ask your vet or breeder to show you procedures that are appropriate for your pet.

Training

While formal obedience is generally best deferred until the sixth month, much groundwork can be laid during puppyhood. This is especially true in terms of bonding and attitude building.

Precisely when to start formal training depends upon the animal's temperament and maturity, and upon the trainer's abilities and experience. Commencing at too young an age can do more harm than good. A puppy who experiences fright during a critical developmental period, whether it be of a collar, of a leash or—God forbid—of you, will never outgrow the feeling, regardless of ensuing positive learning experiences. Clarence Pfaffenberger quotes J. Paul Scott, Ph.D.:

> It is important to remember that, while previous learning may be altered by subsequent learning, subsequent learning will never obliterate previous learning.*

Until you discern some maturation in the young one—such as a lengthened attention span—allow the puppy to be a puppy.

In other words, if in doubt, don't.

*J. Paul Scott, Ph.D., as quoted by Clarence Pfaffenberger in *The New Knowledge of Dog Behavior* (New York: Howell Book House, Inc., 1963), p. 132. This book is an excellent source for further information about *critical periods*.

Puppy Obedience Classes

I have mixed feelings about the concept of puppy obedience classes. They are fine as a socialization vehicle, but that potential is offset by their inherent risk for spreading disease.

From a training standpoint, they can easily be detrimental. For instance, in many classes a puppy is taught he may ignore or respond to his owner's Sit command (for example), as no meaningful compulsion is used to backup the command. The problem is that "Sit" does not mean, "Smack your butt onto the ground, then hop up and do whatever you please," though without enforcement that is how a pup typically responds when made to sit, especially when among peers.

A professed puppy-class goal is to demonstrate obedience is a fun and pleasant activity. This sounds good on paper, but two problems exist. First, this positive attitude should be a constant: It should be operative in any training program, without regard for the animal's age. Second, while it is true that no puppy should be pressured—inappropriate force can scare him at a time when he is highly vulnerable—it is equally true that no dog should ever be taught that a command allows a choice on his part, especially during the impressionable phase of puppyhood.

Puppy-class supporters promote the view that corrections—force—are added to the program when the pooch is old enough to handle them. That's mixed signals and that's my objection. From a training standpoint, to initially demonstrate that commands are open to a vote, and then later change the rules, can instill confusion and distrust in any animal.

Unintended Lessons

Consider the following example of subtle training that can take place inadvertently. While reassurance can be helpful with some children, it is a sure way to cause apprehension and anxiety in a dog. For instance, should a sudden sound cause puppy to startle, ignore both the noise and his anxiety. Rushing to him with, "It's all right, don't worry," and so forth, may only reinforce his nervous reaction to sudden noises. Yes, pet the animal as you normally would if he comes to you, but no, don't fly to him with the express purpose of reassurance. Stable canines have no built-in fear of thunder—it is a natural phenomenon and dogs are beings of nature—but many owners have educated their pets to fear loud noises. A dog's reaction to pointless reassurance is, "If everything's so fine and dandy, then just what are *you* so concerned about?" If a given sound does not worry you, do not teach your pet to fear it.

You're Always on Stage

Along that line of thinking, remember that whenever you are near your companion, even if you are not actively engaged with pup at the moment, you are in fact teaching him, whether you mean to be or not. Be aware, and be careful.

Collars

Regardless of the type of collar you prefer, *be sure* to remove it from your pet's neck when you are not going to be nearby for a while— even for a few minutes! A curious and adventuresome puppy can discover myriad ways of catching a collar on something. Such happenings are usually traumatic and can easily be fatal.

The Play Toy

When playing with a puppy, use tennis balls, laundered burlap sacks, Frisbees—whatever seems to turn the puppy on. Regardless of your toy selection, do not leave the special play toy lying around where the pup can see it, lest the article lose its attraction. If the toy is always present, it can lose its specialness—a puppy can easily learn to take the object for granted. It is only to appear when you do, and then only sometimes. The idea is for the pup to learn to associate the pleasurable object with you.

The few rules governing the proper use of play articles come under the heading of "A Puppy Cannot Do Anything Wrong with a Play Toy." That is, if he is interested in the thrown ball, fine. Should he give chase and pounce upon it, fine. If he picks it up and runs away from you with it, fine. If he goes to the bathroom on it, fine. He cannot do anything improper with a play toy—that is simply not possible. Sending any negative messages that a puppy could infer as relating to the play item can easily lessen his attraction to the object.

To instill and heighten puppy's interest in a play toy, begin by kneeling next to him. (The dominating pressure imparted by body language when standing over a young animal can distract from the moment—in general, things above a dog seize his attention.) Roll the ball back and forth, staring pointedly at the object while observing the pup's reactions peripherally. As he develops interest, move the article to the side of your leg so he will look for the toy. As puppy fascination increases, allow him to pounce upon and carry off the object to the accompaniment of your expressed approval.

The objective is to tempt the puppy with a play toy until he displays strong attraction to it. Making capture of the article easy can cause lost interest for want of challenge and stimulation. At the same time, do not prolong the teasing to an extent that desire wanes. That could teach a pup to lose.

When playing with very young or inexperienced animals, roll a ball for them rather than throwing it. Until a young dog has had some practice in pursuing an object, he is unable to follow visually the flight of a thrown ball, and can easily become confused or frustrated to the extent of losing interest. Field and depth of vision expand with maturity.*

If you are working with several puppies, merely dropping a play toy in their vicinity creates much enticement. One pup will grab the object (if for no other reason than to prevent another from doing so), and the game is begun. If you have an older dog who enjoys chasing a ball, allow the pups to watch from a safe distance, preferably from behind a fence so they cannot interfere with the activity (and perhaps be snapped at). The idea here is to stimulate interest and heighten the desire to participate.

Praise

When your puppy does something that pleases you, tell him. For example, when he trots back to you with *his* ball, pet and praise the young one repetitively, saying, "Good Bring." Do not be in a hurry to take the object from him, lest he learn to come with his head lowered—or not to come at all. When you do take the article, immediately throw it again. Do not tease excessively first—take the toy, wave it in front of his nose a time or two and throw it. Dogs enjoy pursuit as much as they do possession. The purposes are to show your pet that it is in his interests to release the toy to you and to keep his eyes on you afterward.

*Canines are born nearsighted. This is a survival mechanism, as puppies could otherwise be visually drawn from the protection of the nest toward situations that could prove injurious or even life-threatening.

When petting a puppy, especially one with erect ears, confine the fondling to under the chin and along the underside of the neck and muzzle. The idea is to teach your pet to look up at you. This manner of touching is especially important with regard to outsiders whom you allow to pet your animal. Petting a canine atop the head can cause him to lower it while pulling down his ears submissively, and it is unwise to suggest a mind-set of automatic submission toward strangers. Friendliness and curiosity, yes; submission, no.

Identifiers

Assign names to things for your puppy. In addition to their command vocabularies, my dogs have an understanding of objects and concepts numbering another forty-odd terms. Some handy words are: *outside, yard, car, truck, house, chair, couch, bed, nest,* (food) *dish, dinner* (feeding time), *drink, ball, lead, collar, sack* (burlap), *rabbit, horse, bird, critter* (bovine), *deer, warm* and *cold.*

Protection

Prudence dictates taking precautions for your pup's well-being and safety. One of these is an area securely fenced to a minimum height of five feet. That may seem excessive if yours is a small dog, but keep in mind that while a fence is intended to contain your pal, it is also to keep intruders out. There are those who are disposed to taking things that do not belong to them, your pooch included.

Two other safeguards are a watchful eye and no patience with anyone who attempts to tease your pet. Dogs possessing even minimum intelligence and spirit seldom tolerate such abuse for long, and they should not have to.

Do not tie a dog. The practice can easily induce paranoia (as well as an aggressive attitude) since the animal's primary defense—the ability to run away—has been taken from him. Also, tying can create distrust toward yourself, as it is you who have done the taking.

Discourage the behavior of cretinous types who seem compelled to act in an agitating or teasing manner when finding themselves near a Doberman Pinscher, German Shepherd Dog, Rottweiler or any other large dog. Similarly, waste no patience on the clown who habitually ridicules smaller members of the canine world. Such a person's frail ego may need the stimulation, but pooch's spirit should be your first concern.

On a related theme, I never take my dogs off-leash to a public area, regardless of the animal's age or depth of training. I don't ever want to find myself in a courtroom, trying to phrase a disarming reply to the learned judge's query, "Has the dog been trained to bite?" The fact that the child was nipped while trying to stick the animal in the eye may prove a shallow defense. Irrespective of whether your dog has been bite-trained, keep him on-leash whenever the two of you are out in public, lest some yahoo winds up owning your house.

In Closing

I offer the following thoughts, which are adapted from the "Ten Commandments" of the software program *Canis*, and are used with permission from Centron Software Technologies, Inc.

My life is likely to last ten to fifteen years. Any separation from you will be painful for me. Remember that before you buy me.

Give me time to understand what you want of me.

Place your trust in me—it's crucial to my well-being.

Don't be angry at me for long, and don't lock me up as punishment. You have your work, your entertainment and your friends. I have only you.

Talk to me sometimes. Even if I don't understand your words, I understand your voice when it's speaking to me.

Be aware that however you treat me I'll never forget it.

Remember before you hit me that I have teeth that could easily crush the bones of your hand but that I choose not to bite you.

Before you scold me for being uncooperative, obstinate or lazy, ask yourself if something might be bothering me. Perhaps I'm not getting the right food, or I've been out in the sun too long, or my heart is getting old and weak.

Take care of me when I get old; you too will grow old.

Go with me on difficult journeys. Never say, "I can't bear to watch it," or, "Let it happen in my absence." Everything is easier for me if you are there. Remember, I love you.

Boarding?

The breeding section's final topic concerns commercial boarding. Even though you may periodically have room to handle boarders, think twice before bringing strangers' dogs into your kennel. The presence of new dogs in the area is stressful for those already in residence, and there is always the chance of someone's pet bringing disease or parasites to your facility. Understand: I am not saying that boarding is perforce out of the question for breeders; I am suggesting that the costs of boarding can be higher than one might suspect.

TRAINERS

Training facilities are generally akin to boarding kennels in terms of physical layout and responsibilities. The biggest difference is purpose: Instead of merely maintaining someone's pet for just a few days, dogs are often at a training kennel for extended periods, and the animals are being trained as well as boarded. Accordingly, trainers should read the entire *Boarding Kennels* section of this book.

Equipment Storage

When designing your kennels, especially the storeroom area, be certain to allow ample room for equipment. I am not referring to such equipment as jumps, scaling walls and the like—large items can be kept outdoors—but to leashes, collars, long lines, throw chains, dumbbells and protection gear (assuming you train guard dogs) such as body suits, sleeves and so forth.

Training Yard

A primary consideration when planning a training kennel is room for and location of a training area. In that regard, if you have a limited amount of real estate, it is preferable to locate the kennel building so that one large section of property is left for training purposes, rather than configuring the overall layout so that two or three small areas of land are available as training yards. Simply put, one large area— measuring at least one hundred feet square—offers more flexibility for covering different training aspects than do several small yards.

The training yard should be surrounded by a high fence (six to eight feet) that cannot be easily climbed. Gates should be locked when the area is not in use. There should be a few shade trees in or adjacent to the site, and if you plan to do night training, exterior lighting should be installed at least in one area of the yard.

Whether the training yard should be visible from the kennels is

A large training area adjacent to the kennels.

an important consideration. Some trainers feel that dogs learn better by being able to watch other animals being worked; others opine that such a policy knocks down the spirits of dogs who are temporarily "left behind" while others are being trained. My view is that the audience effect is beneficial for all concerned, especially in terms of motivation: The animal being trained is "on stage," getting an opportunity to show the others how it should be done, and the dogs observing are getting psyched up for their chance to perform.

If you prefer to isolate your training yard from the kennel, an obvious solution is erection of a wooden fence. The drawback to such a fence, of course, is that it must be painted or stained every so often, and it can be chewed and may be easy to climb.

Forms and Records

Many of the forms presented in the *Boarding Kennels* section of *Kennels and Kenneling* can be adapted to training kennel use. For example, consider the following *Training Record* and *Training Contract* for use with dogs who are taken for on-leash obedience training.

34

Kennel Name

Training Record

_____   _____
          (Owner)   (Call Name)

_____   _____
          (Address)   (Breed)

                           at
_____   _____ at _____ ____ ____
    (City, State, Zip)   (Age)   (Date)   (Sex) (Alt)

_____   _____
        (Telephone)   (Veterinarian)

_____
       (Medical Problems, Allergies, etc.)

  Shots: Rabies   Distemper   Parvo   Corona   Kennel Cough

Food—Kennel's: _____   Amount per Feeding (Cups):
Food—Owner's: _____   AM_____   N_____   PM_____   E_____

IN Date/Time	OUT Date/Time	Clr	Lsh	Bed	Food	Med	Other	Charges

Training notes: _____

_____

_____

_____

_____

_____

_____

_____

TRAINING CONTRACT

This is a Contract between [Kennel Name] and the pet Owner.

Kennel agrees to exercise due and reasonable care, and to keep the kennel premises sanitary and properly enclosed.

The dog(s) is (are) to be fed properly and regularly, and to be housed in clean, safe quarters.

All dogs are boarded or are otherwise handled or cared for by Kennel staff without liability on Kennel's part for loss or damage from disease, theft, fire, death, escape, injury or harm to persons, other dogs or property by said dog(s), or for other unavoidable causes, due diligence and care having been exercised.

Obedience training will cover on-leash commands to sit, heel, sit automatically during heeling when the handler stops moving, lie down, come when called and to jump over an obstacle. Play-type retrieving will be taught to those dogs who, in the Kennel's sole judgment, show a pronounced instinct for such activity. Owner agrees to pay to Kennel [fee, in numbers] ([fee, in words]) per pet for such training.

All charges incurred by Owner shall be payable upon pickup of pet(s). Owner further agrees that pet(s) shall not leave the Kennel until all charges are paid to Kennel by Owner. Owners of pet(s) left at the Kennel beyond the agreed pickup date will be charged for boarding pet(s) at a rate of [rate, in numbers] ([rate, in words]) per day until pet(s) is claimed.

Kennel shall have, and is hereby granted, a lien on the pet(s) for any and all unpaid charges resulting from boarding and/or training pet(s) at Kennel.

If the pet(s) becomes ill or if the state of the animal's health otherwise requires professional attention, Kennel, in its sole discretion, may engage the services of a veterinarian of its choosing, or administer medicine, or give other requisite attention to the animal, and the expenses thereof shall be paid by Owner.

It is understood by Kennel and Owner that all provisions of this Contract shall be binding upon both parties thereunto for this visit and for all subsequent visits.

This Contract contains the entire agreement between the parties.

_____   _____
(Owner)   (Date)

_____   _____
(Kennel)   (Date)

As you see, the primary difference between the *Training Contract* form and its cousin presented in the *Boarding Kennels* section is the wording, the *Training Contract* detailing the training the dog is to receive, and stating that owners who leave animals beyond the scheduled pickup date will be charged at the current boarding rate.

Visitation Rights

Owners sometimes ask if they can visit their dog during the time the animal is with you for training. While there are trainers who have no problem with such a request—moreover, some encourage the idea—my practice is summarized in the phrase "No way!" An owner showing up for a few hours now and then not only disrupts my day generally and my training schedule specifically, it is very hard on the dog: The animal cannot understand why he has to stay behind when the owner leaves. It is difficult enough to get an animal settled for the demands of training without periodic appearances by any member of the dog's family. The effect of such visits—which makes more sense in people terms than in dog terms—is to distract the animal after the fact for several days.

The Big Day

As *Kennels and Kenneling* is not a book about breeding, neither is it a training manual. Still, I would be ducking an issue were I not to outline general procedures related to dealing with owners, especially in terms of turning over a trained dog to an excited client.

An owner has arrived to collect his or her pet. You have spent some time visiting with the individual, detailing the dog's training, summarizing how the animal has fared, discussing certain training basics. Today is the day pooch is going home. But don't let the dog know that. Not yet, anyway.

My practice, after meeting with the owner, is to leave the individual at a place where he or she can see the training yard but which is downwind and some distance from it. I then go leash up pooch, and work the animal with the owner looking on. I caution the client ahead of time to make no sounds or movements that might catch the dog's attention. I then bring the animal to the owner and for the next few minutes—as I earlier told the person would be the case—all bets are off. Sure, the dog could be made to hold a Sit-Stay, for instance, while the owner greets the dog, but that is not obedience, it's cruelty. If the dog is a large animal I am not going to let him knock his owner flat, but at the same time reasonable displays of joy and affection at reunion are not going to be thwarted.

After a few minutes I hand the owner the leash and tell him or her something like, "Here are the keys; now, let's see you work your dog." My role then becomes one of teacher while I watch the team go through various paces. As the objective is not to turn the owner into a trainer but a handler of a trained dog, once it is apparent that the individual has a few basic concepts in mind and seems at ease working his or her dog, it is time they were on their way. A person can only absorb so many new ideas in a given period of time, and the dog can only be worked for so long without becoming tired or bored. To help the owner along in his acquisition of training skills and concepts, I present him or her with a copy of the following list of training basics (which, like the *Having to do with Puppies* booklet, you are welcome to retype and distribute as you wish, provided you credit this book and its publisher as the source).

SOME TRAINING HINTS

Work daily with your dog for fifteen to twenty minutes. Two daily sessions are best, with several hours between each. Don't train sooner than an hour after feeding your pet, or he might work sluggishly or experience cramping. The animal should be given an ample opportunity to relieve himself before work or play begins.

If you work with pooch for twenty minutes a day, you should also play with him for a like period every day. Playtime is kept separate from work periods for now, although the training collar is to be worn during either activity. There are to be *no* commands given during play periods. The play object must be put away from your dog's sight after playtime. If it is not removed, and instead is left to lay around, its attraction to an animal lessens greatly.

Initial teaching of new lessons takes place in a distraction-free area. Distractions are gradually introduced only after it is evident that learning has taken place. Play objects you may wish to later use in teaching different work should not initially be used as distractions. Some good distractions are other animals, people, traffic settings and bitches in season. Gunfire at reasonable distances is appropriate conditioning for most dogs.

Family members may be present during practice (but not during the actual teaching of any new work), but they should neither use your pet's name, nor should they establish eye contact with him. Do not use your dog's food dish as a distraction, nor a stranger who appears to be of a threatening or oddly-behaving type.

Let your pooch know that it is a given that you are the leader (of the pack), and that you enjoy both his companionship and the work and play sessions. Carefully plan each period, anticipating how your dog may perform and how you will respond.

Give *one* clear, decisive command, and proceed with no hesitation in your next move. Employ commands only when you mean to, and do not give commands that you cannot immediately backup physically. The dog's name is not used when giving commands; it is sometimes used during praise; it is *never* used during correction.

Praise and correction are two basic ways of showing a dog where his advantage lies. Be consistent with each in such a manner that he is made aware that it is *his* actions (or lack thereof) which causes one to occur over the other.

Verbally praise your dog according to what he has just done, as with, "Good Sit," "Good Bring," "Good Stay" and so forth, as contrasted with, "Good boy," "Good dog" and the like.

Just as affection is not a component of praise, anger has no useful purpose in correction.

Avoid looming over your dog when praising him, and do not pound on him as a form of affection. Pet calmly and speak quietly, communicating affirmation rather than affection. Affection should be given a dog throughout his life—he should not have to work for it.

Refrain from working at any one exercise for so long that you actually guarantee your pet a correction. That attitude teaches a dog to lose.

Do not dwell on a correction (except in response to trainer-directed aggression); apply it properly and move on. *Never* correct a dog who is frightened or confused.

Vary the times and locations of your practice sessions, working indoors as well as out, and in all reasonable forms of weather.

The time for effective training is not when you are tired or ill, or when you are pressed for time or are irritated.

For the first few weeks your dog should have one trainer: You.

Improper aggression from your pet is not to be tolerated, ever.

Smokers should avoid their habit during working/play sessions.

End each period on a positive note, with your pooch having just performed an exercise successfully.

Do not involve your dog in any other activity (including feeding) immediately following training. Rather, encourage the passage of some quiet, contemplative time.

NEVER ALLOW AN UNSUPERVISED DOG TO WEAR ANY COLLAR!

The length of time of the reuniting process varies from owner to owner, but you should count on spending at least a couple of hours with the client from the time he or she arrives to get the dog.

Boarding?

Should you offer the service in addition to training? If you have the time and interest to do a proper job of it, my thought is "Why not?" You can garner extra income, and you may be able to talk some of the owners into availing their pets of your training services. Just be sure to remember that boarding a dog takes time, and that no animal should be neglected in favor of other activities. Also, realize that boarding can—in some instances—lower your income. Suppose you have a full kennel and someone contacts you about training. You would like to take the individual's dog right away, but the run in which you would house the animal is in use by a boarder who is scheduled to be with you for several weeks. If the caller decides that he does not want to wait until you can take his dog, and contacts another trainer, that's money out of your pocket because you can make a good deal more from training a dog than for boarding one.

Reflection

Every dog is a lion at home.

Torriano, *Piazza Universale*, 36 (1666)

SECTION II

Boarding Kennels

3

Planning, Design and Construction

T HE TOUGHEST QUESTION I had to answer in planning my kennel was "Which question do I deal with first?" When considering several separate yet related variables—size of operation, location, overall layout, the building's design, heating, cooling, plumbing and waste-disposal systems, electrical wiring, security fencing, landscaping—the list can become so overwhelming that knowing where to begin may seem difficult.

Further, each general category consists of subtopics. Consider, for example, a few questions pertaining to something as basic and ostensibly simple as runs. What surface is best? Gravel, dirt, concrete or some other material? How many runs should there be? What direction should they face? What size should the runs be? Should they all be the same size? Should the runs be separated by some material other than fencing? If so, what kind of material? But if fencing is used, what type is preferable? Chain-link? Woven wire? Non-climb? Something else? Is fencing needed across the tops of the runs?

As you see, a great many important decisions await you. The functions of this chapter are to help you determine the questions you need to address, and to provide options and planning techniques for your consideration.

PLANNING

Building Permits and Zoning Restrictions

The first step in the planning process is to visit with the powers that be in your town in charge of such matters as issuing building permits, and determine who you are going to have to keep happy about what. If you are fortunate enough to live on what is generally termed "unrestricted land," you are in for a much easier time than if you reside in an area having a proliferation of building regulations, zoning restrictions and covenants controlled by ubiquitous bureaucrats. Regardless of your locale and what you "think" you know about its land laws, do some legwork and find out what—if anything—you are up against, and how to satisfy the system while still getting the job done in terms of building your kennel.

A related consideration concerns looking for property upon which to build both a home and a kennel. If you are in the market for real estate, seek at least a semi-isolated setting; consider your proposed site relative to population. You may find a location where establishing a kennel is legal but which is also quite near a residential area. Though no restrictions may exist that would hamper your objective, it would be wiser as well as more considerate to seek a more remote area. Perhaps you would not be violating any laws or regulations by building your kennel in or near a populated area, but you might well incur sufficient ill will from local residents to harm your business.

Inspections

In your locale, are there regulations pertaining to examinations that have to be made by certified regulators before you can do business? If you do not know, find out, and make sure that your facility is in compliance.

What Size?

This is a candle-and-flame type of decision, as "What Size?" is related, even dependent upon "Where?" No purpose is served by planning a thirty-run facility if you have room only for ten. My steps for answering "What Size?" begin by determining the size of a single outdoor run.

1) To afford adequate space for a large dog to exercise and maneuver, what size should your outside runs be? (As outdoor runs require more space than indoor ones, they are the primary consideration in allotment of space.) Mine are sixteen feet long by four feet wide, which seems to be ample. The dimensions may seem restrictive for housing an Irish Wolfhound, for example, but remember that the nature of a boarding kennel presupposes that it houses occupants temporarily, not permanently. Also, consider that should you have to deal with an aggressive animal, there is a thin line between limiting how much of a rush you want him to be able to take at you versus providing adequate room for yourself to maneuver. Of course, if you plan to board only small dogs, runs sixteen feet in length by four feet in width may be about eight feet too long and a foot too wide.

2) Should all outdoor runs be the same size? There is a school of thought among some boarding kennel people that says it is wise to construct runs of two basic sizes. The rationale behind this thinking is that seldom will one's kennel be filled totally by large dogs. Since a percentage of the runs will often be occupied by small animals, why not save on construction costs by making some of the runs small?

Though there is some merit to that argument, my preference is to have all large runs. True, I rarely have a kennel full of big dogs, but it does happen. By limiting the size of some of my runs I am limiting the number of large dogs I can *properly* house. Yes, a Newfoundland will survive a few days of being boarded in a small run, but that isn't the point. That Newf—or any other dog—is entitled to comfort, which the "sardine can" effect of too much dog in too little space does not provide.

3) Once you have determined the size of your outside runs, decide how many runs your kennel should have. The first factor in this equation is the size of your property: Does it limit the number of runs your facility can have? If so, how many runs do you have room for? Note this number—mark it "Space for"—and set it aside for a moment.

4) If space imposes no restrictions, how many runs can you service daily? Assuming a maximum occupancy of two dogs per run, how many runs can you gracefully deal with? Write down this number—mark it "Serviceable runs"—and set it aside.

5) Which number is less, "Space for" or "Serviceable runs"? That is tentatively the number of runs your kennel should have. If you have room for thirty runs, for example, but sense that you do not have the time to properly deal with more than twenty runs daily, twenty is the number to hang onto for the moment. Mark this number "Tentative." We will come back to it momentarily.

6) This last can be the trickiest variable in the formula. Answer the question "How many runs do you think you could sell on an average day once your business has built up a clientele, a following?" If you have difficulty pinning down a number, visit with other local dog folk and put the question to them, asking them to respond as though they were planning a boarding kennel. Talk with enough people who are sincere in giving you their best guesstimates, and in time you will start to notice a commonality among their responses. Why? Because they are local dog people, and as such they have a feel for what the needs are in your locale. They have a sense, an awareness, of the potential, even if they have never consciously pondered the question. Once you have concluded your informal survey, the likelihood is that the number mentioned most often will be very close to the one you had settled on, perhaps without even realizing you had. It will sound "right" to you.

In any case, let's say the number is twelve. Your gut feeling, and that of your friends, is that once your enterprise gets rolling, you will be able to fill a dozen runs daily. Now multiply that number by two. Remember, we are asking how many runs you could sell on an *average* day. Some days you will have fewer runs occupied, some days more, and my experience is that I fill about twice as many runs during peak periods than during average days. Hence, the multiplier factor of two, which in this example leads us to a need for twenty-four runs. Note that number and mark it "Peak Demand."

Is this a foolproof formula for projecting demand, one that is a product of cold analytical study, resplendent in phrases such as "demographic analysis" and "computer modeling"? Hardly. Some might feel that it is laughable. But it is rooted in the simple fact that without spending a small fortune on professional surveys and the like, you have to go with your reading of your area to answer the question "How many runs can I fill daily once my business is established?" This estimate can best be enhanced by the opinions of other area dog people who are likely to have a good feel for the demand where they live. Then that number of runs is doubled to lessen the incidence of turndowns during busier times of the year.

46

7) Compare that last number—twenty-four, which you labeled "Peak Demand"—with the one you earlier marked "Tentative," which was twenty. Plan your kennels on the basis of having twenty runs. True, we have concluded that four more runs could be filled during high-demand times of the year, but twenty runs are all you feel you can handle. Had our "What can we sell daily?" analysis resulted in seven runs, for instance, we would plan on the facility having fourteen runs (seven times two). You can handle twenty runs a day, yes, but the market will only support fourteen at best, so there is no point in constructing the six extra runs.

Consider one final factor pertaining to run count. Let's say that our analysis fixes fourteen runs as your bottom-line number. Round that number to fifteen. Why? Because many commercial suppliers of chain-link kennels—which is the best material for the money for a boarding kennel—routinely prefabricate run gates in banks of five. The cost difference of prefabricated gate panels versus that of individual gates can be significant, enough so that you may be money ahead to absorb the cost of constructing a fifteenth run even though you had determined that fourteen runs was the optimal number. Remember, too, that our calculations of "How many runs should I build?" is seat-of-the-pants in nature, and a margin of error of plus-or-minus one or two runs is acceptable.

In each section, when comparing two numbers pertaining to how many runs to build, I have recommended choosing the lower number. This comes from my err-on-the-side-of-caution tendency in dealing with dog-related issues, from how firmly to initiate discipline to how many runs to erect. Just as a trainer can always get tougher with a given dog should the need exist, design your kennel so that there is little risk of overbuilding, but in such a way that it can be expanded.

Yes, the cautious approach can seem tedious and unexciting at times, but consider that if one does expand a facility later, after business results have demonstrated that demand is greater than supply, the kennel operator will be in a position to add on using other people's (clients') money; additions will be paid for from profits, not from original capital.

Don't Shackle Yourself

As suggested, do incorporate room for growth into your original design. Even if you do not envision ever expanding the kennel, it is unwise to restrict today what you might change your mind about tomorrow. True, a kennel having a certain number of runs may be as large as you will ever want to operate, but what if you someday decide to sell the operation? Suppose there is a buyer who would meet your price except that he or she wants to increase the number of runs and sees that the design of your kennel would make it cost-prohibitive to do so. Or, suppose that you someday decide that you wish to add sales of equipment or food to your operation. Is your planned storeroom large enough to handle an inventory of such items? Those are but two reasons why it is better to not limit tomorrow's options today. Leaving room for change is one bull's-eye to hit the first time.

Bottom Line

The point of all this is that when planning a major installation like a boarding kennel, you need to get it as right as possible the first time. "Should," "probably," "maybe," "good enough" and "That might work" are words and phrases that have no place in the planning, design or construction of a kennel, any more than they do in the designing and building of a house. True, many design faults can be corrected after construction, but it is a good deal less stressful on your budget (and on you) to get it right initially.

DESIGN

Configuration

How do you envision the overall layout of your kennel? Will it have runs on only one side of the building? On two sides? Three? On all four? Concepts to factor into your decision are *centralization*, the *best use of available space*, *security* and your area's *weather*, though not necessarily in that order.

What is meant by *centralization*? Consider an extreme example of noncentralization: a four-run kennel having one run on each of the building's four sides. Sure, that is a ludicrous configuration, but by implication it illustrates the principle of centralization. Runs scattered about a building are impractical, if for no other reason than an inordinate amount of time would be spent going from run to run just to clean them. Properly centralized, the four runs would be side by side on one side of the building. Quick cleaning would then be facilitated as the operator could go from one run to the next.

Best use of available space is akin to the concept of centralization, although the two can be at odds with one another. Visualize a ten-run kennel having all ten runs on one side of the building. That is a centralized configuration, alright, but it may not represent the best use of available space: Three sides of the building are unused. Such a layout may be appropriate in some situations, as when the kennel building serves more than a single purpose and the other sides are better used for other functions. When discussing a structure that is intended solely as a boarding kennel, however, it is preferable to use the entire building. Accordingly, were I designing a ten-run facility, I would locate five runs on each of two sides and would place a storeroom on one of the remaining two ends and leave the other wall open for access and for possible future expansion.

Though the best use of available space and centralization concepts should be kept uppermost in your mind during the design process, a principle of equal importance is *security*. By security I refer to such notions as having multiple exterior doors for fire-escape purposes. Installing locks on those doors, erecting a perimeter fence around the kennel area and locating the facility such that all outside runs are visible from your house are other examples of security, as are run gates that can be padlocked, a fence around your property (this is in addition to the perimeter fence surrounding the kennel area), a motion sensor in the storeroom, smoke detectors and fire extinguishers throughout the building, installing all electrical outlets and switches higher than most dogs can reach and surrounding the kennel building with wide walkways of shale, gravel or a similar substance that is noisy when trod upon, making it difficult if not impossible for an intruder to approach the facility without alerting its occupants (whose barking would alert you).

The fourth factor to consider is *weather*. Runs should be located so that none continually takes the brunt of summer heat or prevailing winter winds. Yes, all runs should receive some of the sun's rays daily—sunlight is an excellent disinfectant—but no run should be exposed to perpetual, cook-an-egg-on-its-surface heat. Does this mean that south-facing runs cannot be erected? No. It means that runs can be pointed in any direction you want, provided you install overhead sunscreens and erect windbreaks, and/or have trees for shade and to impede winter's blasts.

Even allowing for the foregoing constraints, overall kennel configuration is limited only by one's imagination. Following is a rough floor plan for a ten-run facility. It is not offered with the message that it is inherently better or more complete than one you might come up with; it is simply a possibility, presented to give you ideas.

		Door			
Outdoor Run #1	1		6	Outdoor Run #6
Outdoor Run #2	2	L	7	Outdoor Run #7
Outdoor Run #3	3		8	Outdoor Run #8
Outdoor Run #4	4	L	9	Outdoor Run #9
Outdoor Run #5	5		10	Outdoor Run #10

H S   Door   F

Door   L   Door   ↑ N

Cage   Food

Door

The numbered squares adjacent to each outdoor run mark the indoor runs. The storeroom is the area having four doors, wherein "H" represents a hot-water heater, "S" means sink, "F" symbolizes a furnace, "L" stands for overhead lighting fixtures throughout the building. Shelving could be installed on any of the storeroom walls, except in the area used by the furnace. Office and/or grooming space can be added merely by increasing the size of the storeroom. Note how easily this layout could be expanded (page 51).

Note, too, that the size of the storeroom would likely have to be expanded because of the increased number of runs.

I Can Barely Draw a Straight Line, but . . .

I am fortunate to know more than one person who can create accurate images on paper. Such folks were a godsend when I was planning my kennel, and hopefully you are either talented or willing, or you know someone who is. It is one thing to mentally conceive several ideas around a central theme; it is another to visualize the composite result with sufficient accuracy that you can confidently proceed to the construction phase.

First, draw your plans as best you can, specifying all dimensions. Then, unless you are good at graphic design and representation, engage the services of someone who can work from your sketches and make your ideas come to life on paper.

```
                          Door
┌────────────────────┬───┐         ┌───┬────────────────────┐
│ Outdoor  Run  #1   │ 1 │         │ 6 │ Outdoor  Run  #6   │
├────────────────────┼───┤         ├───┼────────────────────┤
│ Outdoor  Run  #2   │ 2 │    L    │ 7 │ Outdoor  Run  #7   │
├────────────────────┼───┤         ├───┼────────────────────┤
│ Outdoor  Run  #3   │ 3 │         │ 8 │ Outdoor  Run  #8   │
├────────────────────┼───┤         ├───┼────────────────────┤
│ Outdoor  Run  #4   │ 4 │    L    │ 9 │ Outdoor  Run  #9   │
├────────────────────┼───┤         ├───┼────────────────────┤
│ Outdoor  Run  #5   │ 5 │         │ 10│ Outdoor  Run  #10  │
└────────────────────┴───┘         └───┴────────────────────┘
                         H S    Door      F
                                                              ↑
             Door           L          Door                  N
                 Cage          Food
```

H S   Door   F

L

Cage   Food

Door

Location

Once you have decided how many runs your kennel will have and have created at least a rough sketch of the facility, it is time to determine location. This could be the first step, as you perhaps already have a general notion where you will build. But until you have determined the number of runs, which contributes to settling the kennel's overall size, selecting an exact site is difficult.

A primary consideration is the presence of trees. They can not only lend a restful, aesthetically pleasing quality to your operation, they can provide shade, security and windbreaks, and act as a sound deadener, depending on how you locate your building relative to their positions. Thus, if you have more than one possible site on which to erect your facility, use the area near the most trees. Locate the kennel runs to take advantage of the trees' blessings in the pecking order given above: shade, security, windbreak, sound suppression.

In planning to use the amenities your trees afford, remember that they represent a trade-off. Trees create natural debris and make for extra cleaning chores during the spring and fall. Generally speaking, trees in the kennel area are well worth any extra effort for the reasons given. The final decision must be yours.

CONSTRUCTION AND MATERIALS

Walls

For my money the optimal material for constructing exterior kennel walls is eight-inch concrete block, reinforced with half-inch steel rebar and filled with concrete; six-inch block can be used for interior, non-load-bearing walls. Concrete block is fireproof, readily available, adaptable, affordable, can be packed with granular insulation and with proper reinforcement is virtually dog-proof in terms of indestructibility. It is true that concrete-block porosity can make for a germ haven, but it is equally true that a properly applied coating of block-filler (which produces a semi-smooth surface) followed by multiple coats of industrial-grade enamel or acrylic paint can greatly obviate that risk.

Another benefit to concrete-block buildings, especially those that are sealed with paint, is that they contain sound well. That can be a minus when you are in the building at a time when several boarders decide to harmonize, but it is a plus from a neighbor's point of view and—long-term—that is a plus for you.

A drawback to concrete-block construction is that you may have to hire a professional to do the work. It is not only the weight of the blocks that necessitates skilled help, it is the fact that each block has to be positioned just so or a person can wind up with a leaning tower of kennel. Blocks can be incorrectly placed any number of ways, and a recurring fraction-of-an-inch error starting at the foundation level can expand to a glitch of several inches by the roof line.

A material to avoid in wall construction is wood. Not only is it vulnerable to fire, even the hardest wood is not impervious to canine chewing or clawing. Wood is acceptable for ceiling and roof construction, provided the ceiling is painted with several coats of heavy enamel or acrylic paint to retard moisture and germs. Because wood is far more forgiving of slight errors than concrete block, you may be able to do some of the wood work yourself, thereby saving on construction costs.

Some kennel operators are sold on the idea of metal siding. My objections to the material are that it is costly, dents easily, does not

Well-designed and placed kennel windows.

contain sound well, and its appearance is less than pleasing to the eye. Those drawbacks, and the fact that some kinds provide poor insulation against heat and cold, keep me from recommending the material.

Windows

Windows should be mounted high enough above the indoor runs that no dog can reach them. They should be openable, to permit a periodic airing out, and lockable, for security purposes.

Exterior Doors

Insulated metal doors (for people access) are my choice for a boarding kennel. They are durable, affordable, sanitary, and do a good job of keeping the elements at bay, especially given the fact that a magnetic strip installed around the door frame causes the doors to seal more tightly than nonmetal doors. My single objection to insulated metal doors concerns the "metal" part: They can be dented.

Interior Doors

My preference for interior doors, which are often used to separate the indoor run area from a storeroom or office, is wooden Dutch doors

A Dutch door leading from the storeroom to the indoor-kennel area.

sealed with multiple coats of industrial-grade enamel or acrylic paint. Opening the top half of the door during the day promotes better air flow, and facilitates allowing a selected dog to spend some time with you in the storeroom or office while enabling you to keep an eye and ear on the other boarders.

Whatever type of doors you select—for exterior or interior purposes—make them at least three feet wide. Narrower widths are available at less cost, true, but when you are dealing with a large, unruly dog, or are carrying heavy bags of dog food into the kennel, you may appreciate the extra room.

Run Access Doors

At a rate of one door per run, this equipment can quickly add up to a significant investment. Still, security and ease of use must remain foremost considerations, so don't skimp on these items.

The market offers a varied selection of styles and prices, but my preference is for galvanized, vertically sliding doors, often termed "guillotine" doors. Though I abhor the label I like the product for manageability, durability, security and cost. Each door is kept in place by a long, metal, wall-mounted track on each side of the door. Installed

Operated by a chain-pulley system, overhead guillotine doors are my choice for run-access doors.

The ability to lock a run-access door open is a convenience for the dog and for you.

indoors, strong but lightweight chain fed through a pulley above each unit can then be attached to the top of each door, providing you with an easy means of opening and closing the doors without having to enter a run. Further, the doors can easily be locked open by clipping the chain to a spring-loaded lock attached to the top of each corresponding run. This allows boarders to spend time inside or outside according to each dog's individual preference.

A drawback to guillotine doors is that a determined, powerful dog can literally tear them out of their tracks. I have encountered many canines with the ability but few with the inclination, however, and have housed those rare claustrophobic and/or destructive animals in high-security cages at night, allowing them run time during the day and locking their run access doors open.

Regarding the size of the run access doors, there are two considerations: First, the size of the doorways (the actual openings in the wall) should be 14 inches wide by 28½ inches high. These dimensions are adequate for even the largest dogs to gain entry, yet are small enough not to waste heating or air-conditioning efforts. The dimensions of the metal guillotine doors themselves should be in the neighborhood of thirty inches high by sixteen inches wide.

At the bottom of each doorway there should be a solid, concrete-block threshold 4½ inches high, to keep water and snow from the indoor run. This threshold block should be slightly tilted toward the outside run to promote water runoff and drying.

Roofing

In choosing a roofing surface, consider that rolled roofing is far less costly than shingles. It is also easier to apply, perhaps opening the do-it-yourself door. Shingles are more vulnerable to damage, especially from wind, but at the same time they are easier to replace than are sections of rolled roofing. Properly applied, either presents a pleasing appearance.

Ceiling

A plywood ceiling is acceptable in a boarding kennel. The material is inexpensive, durable and reasonably easy to shape and handle. The ceiling should be painted with multiple coats of high-gloss paint to provide an easily cleanable surface that reflects light well.

Flooring

Concrete is the way to go. The material is readily available, durable, easily cleaned and affordable. Its drawbacks are that it is only moderately effective in shutting out heat and cold, and that—like concrete block—it may be necessary to hire skilled labor to pour and finish it. Make certain that reinforcing steel mesh is laid in the formed areas prior to pouring the pads. This technique reduces the likelihood of major cracking.

It may occur to you to paint your flooring. I did, and it was a mistake. Concrete takes paint well enough but paint does not withstand the constant wearing from canine nails. Bare concrete is not very attractive, but it is more so than painted concrete from which the paint has been randomly scratched away.

Interior Lighting

All interior lighting should be mounted on the ceiling. A boarding kennel is not a place for table, pole, or hanging lamps. Not only is there a high risk of breakage, any such accident could injure a boarder. Two hallway-centered, overhead fixtures, each containing one two-hundred-watt bulb, adequately illuminates a fifteen-foot by twenty-foot room. In choosing the style of fixture, the amount of light emitted is of more importance than decor. Accordingly, my preference is for the clear, rounded-end variety that resembles a glass jar. Yes, glass is breakable, but there are few plastic fixtures that can handle the heat generated by two-hundred-watt bulbs.

Exterior Lighting

Though exterior lighting is a convenience, its primary function is security. When cleaning runs after dark it is convenient to be able to see what you are doing—and where you step—but of greater importance is being able to illuminate the kennel and adjacent grounds with the flick of a switch. Wiring should be installed so that the exterior lights can be controlled from the kennel itself and from your house. Again, that is a convenience, but security is still the main purpose.

Inside-Run Dividers

Use six-inch concrete block to separate indoor, side-by-side runs. This way no dog can see another next to him or her, which makes for

Overhead interior lighting. Note the overhead fan suspended between the light fixtures.

A close-up shot of the overhead fan suspended between the interior-lighting fixtures. Surprisingly, this small unit provides adequate air circulation for the entire kennel interior.

a much quieter kennel. Including the exterior wall, this results in each interior run having solid walls on three sides, which provides occupants with a measure of emotional security. They don't feel so exposed, as they would were the indoor runs separated by chain-link, for instance. Boarders can see other animals several feet away through the chain-link, indoor-run gates, which lessens feelings of isolation.

Like the building's exterior and interior walls, the run dividers should be reinforced with half-inch rebar and filled with concrete for maximum strength. Eight-inch concrete blocks could be used as interior-run separators, though doing so would constitute a waste of space and materials. Do not use blocks narrower than six inches, however. No dog could destroy a properly reinforced wall of two-inch blocks, for instance, but a large, powerful canine could significantly damage and perhaps weaken the structure.

Interior runs need be no higher than four feet. Keeping the interior run height low not only makes for much better air flow throughout the kennel building, it makes for a quieter kennel as the boarders are more constrained in their activities. They can get all the jump-around exercise they need when they are outside.

Outside-Run Dividers

Outside runs should be made separate from one another by placing four-feet-high chain-link panels atop two-feet-high dividers fashioned from concrete or four-inch concrete block. The result, of course, is a total run height of six feet. Though it is easily done, chain-link should not be the sole means of separating runs: Liquids can flow from one run to another, and the incidence of fence fighting is much higher. Concrete block or poured concrete dividers eliminates the possibility of liquids flowing to a neighboring run, and they also greatly discourage fence fighting.

The chain-link panels should not merely rest atop the concrete-block (or poured concrete) dividers; they should be attached to them. If the panels are not attached to the dividers, a large, powerful dog could push a panel far enough from a divider that she could catch a paw between the panel and the divider as the panel springs back. Attaching panels to dividers is easily done by looping several inches of plumber's metal strapping tape over a panel's bottom rail, and pressing the ends of the tape into the divider while the concrete is still wet (see photograph). For best results, the spacing of the strapping tape should be every four feet.

Exterior lighting for the kennels and the training yard.

Interior run height should not be greater than four feet.

Outside-run dividers.

Preventing chain-link panel's side-to-side action by attaching the panel to the concrete-block divider.

The market offers metal panels for attaching to the lower part of each panel, thereby separating boarders, but in times of high heat these panels can become quite hot and could possibly burn a dog. Also, though metal panels can alleviate fence fighting, they are ineffective against preventing liquids from flowing from run to run.

Inside-Run Tops

My indoor runs are topped with lightweight fencing stapled to wooden frames made from two-inch by two-inch lumber that matches the dimensions of each run top. The forms are held in place by window locks attached to two-inch by two-inch lumber that separates each run top from the one next to it.

Incidentally, though it may seem a handy location to store large objects (airline cages, for example), it is better to refrain from placing such items onto inside-run tops. Not only would the practice block light from illuminating the run, such objects above a dog would tend to make the animal nervous. Further, it is unwise to place small, lightweight items (such as leashes or blankets) on the run tops, as the run's occupant may attempt to pull the objects into her run as a game. A dog would not be able to do so, of course—the run-top fencing would see to that—but in trying, an animal could damage the item sought, the run top or possibly injure herself in some way.

Outside-Run Overhead Fencing

Why, you may wonder, is it necessary to put fencing across the tops of runs that are six feet high? True, a dog would probably have a heck of a time jumping over such a height, but don't presume that cats are the only house pets who can climb. I have seen more than one dog scramble up a chain-link run panel.

Also, the overhead fencing serves a second security purpose: It lessens the chance that some deranged soul would be successful in hurling a tainted substance (like poisoned meat) into a run.

The fencing I have across my outside runs is lightweight wire mesh that has been attached to the vertical run panels using electric-fence wire, which is strong enough wire for the job yet thin and malleable enough to make working with it easy. It occurred to me to use chain-link tops, but they are expensive and difficult to handle, owing to their weight. Using lightweight wire-mesh fencing may seem inadequate until one realizes that no dog is capable of climbing a chain-link side panel and hanging there for the time it would take to chew through the overhead material.

Run Gates

Run gates—interior and exterior—should be fabricated from chain-link. Their bottom support rails should be raised from the concrete by 2½ inches, to allow sufficient room for hosing solids from the runs into a clean-out trough without creating a situation wherein a large dog could catch a paw under a rail, or from which a small animal could escape. Outdoor gates should be six feet high so you do not have to stoop when entering or departing a run. Indoor gates should be four feet high mounted in six-foot-high frames, with the excess or open part of each frame being above each gate. If six-foot-high gates were used, the area above each interior run would be blocked from your access.

Chain-link Mesh Sizes

Chain-link mesh sizes vary greatly. Too large a mesh can allow a small dog to lodge his head in a square; too small a gap can enable a large dog to catch a paw. Though the "right" size depends upon who you talk to, my preference for a boarding kennel is mesh that is two inches square.

Run Surfacing

Of the three more common types of run surfaces—dirt, gravel and concrete—my preference in boarding kennel construction is concrete, for two reasons: security and ease in cleaning and disinfecting. Security because I have yet to meet a dog who could dig through it, though I have encountered many for whom a dirt or gravel surface presented a challenge if not an outright invitation. Ease in cleaning and disinfecting because, well—can you imagine trying to scrub a graveled or dirt-surfaced run?

A disadvantage to concrete is that it is hard on the legs, joints and feet of dogs confined on it for extended periods. This problem can be circumvented to a degree through the use of resting pads in the indoor runs, and by allowing time in an exercise yard. Another drawback is that the material is more costly than gravel or dirt, especially given the fact that skilled labor may be needed to form the pads, pour them and finish the surface.

Note that there is no need to tightly attach the overhead fencing to the chain-link panel.

Two locks are needed for each gate. The padlock is used when you're going to be off-property for a time. The other lock, which is merely a curved piece of metal inserted in the lock aperture such that a dog cannot dislodge it, is for any other time.

Run surfaces—both interior and exterior—should be sloped away from the kennel walls at the rate of one-quarter inch per foot of length. This ensures that urine and cleaning substances will flow away from the building, but the pitch is not so great as to make for difficult footing, even when runs are wet or icy. The width dimension of the runs should be dead level, to prevent liquids from flowing into adjacent runs. The depth of the concrete should be between four and six inches, depending on winter severity, pad size and the stability of the ground in your area. If you are uncertain, thicker is generally better, but do not go to extremes. Be safe by checking with a local concrete-driveway contractor.

Exterior run surfaces should be configured and poured as a pad, instead of as a separate pour for each run. Pad pours are not only generally easier, they are usually less expensive.

Once you have determined the length and width of your outdoor-run pads, add twelve inches to the overall length and to the overall width. For instance, a pad for five runs, each of which is four feet wide by sixteen feet long, should measure twenty-one feet wide (four feet wide per run times five runs, plus twelve inches) by seventeen feet long (sixteen feet long plus twelve inches). The purpose is to provide a six-inch safety margin from side to side, and a foot of room for a clean-out trough at the end of the runs.

Waste Disposal

Though in some locales public-health dictates may make the decision for you, a common boarding kennel solution to the need for efficient waste disposal is an underground septic system. A clean-out trough at the end of and perpendicular to each series of runs, sloped toward the drain at a rate of one-quarter inch for each foot of length, leads to a drain that empties into a septic tank that drains into a leach field. The septic tank should be periodically pumped out to lessen the strain on it and on the leach system.

To be sure, this is an expensive system, but it can pay for itself over time in saved trash-hauling fees. It also makes for much easier run cleaning. The traditional alternative is surrounding each run pad with a bed of drainage gravel several inches deep into which urine and cleaning solutions are hosed, and scooping or shoveling feces into several large trash cans that have been double-lined with heavy-duty bags. The first time a bag ruptures while being moved, however, resulting in its contents being strewn about, can not only lead one to

An outdoor clean-out trough abutting the run pad, and a hazard: Leaf collection in the drain. Flushed into the system in quantity, they can plug a leach field.

With proper plumbing, septic gasses should not be able to enter the kennel building. A drain cap, like the one shown, makes sure they can't.

ponder dark thoughts, it can induce no less than a longing for the convenience of a septic system.

Perimeter Fencing

Saying that there are more kinds and styles of fences than there are purebred breeds of dogs may overstate the case, but not by much. For surrounding a kennel, however, there are only three good options: chain-link, wire mesh or wood.

Chain-link is durable and adapts well to boarding kennel usage. It is also very expensive and is not the easiest type of fencing to install.

Wire-mesh fencing, especially the non-climb variety, is also durable, easier for most people to install than chain-link, and in addition to being more affordable, it thwarts canine visions of escape as well as chain-link does. Though a droopy non-climb fence would suggest sloppy workmanship, do not stretch perimeter fencing until it is razor tight: Non-climb fencing having a little give is harder for a dog to climb than is one attached as tight as a drumhead.

Stay away from lightweight-gauge, woven-wire fencing. Most

Set gate and corner posts
in concrete for stability and
permanence.

dogs cannot chew through the material, but repeated jumping against it can cause the wires to separate. It is also vulnerable to rusting.

Though any type of wire fencing—chain-link or wire-mesh—does nothing to dampen sound, wooden fence material does. Unfortunately, wooden fences can be vulnerable to chewing, climbing and wind. They also require periodic maintenance in the form of painting or staining.

If the type of fence you choose to erect around your kennels necessitates the use of wooden posts, be sure to use materials that have been either treated against moisture and insects or are naturally impervious to such problems. The only aspect of fencing that is more difficult than original construction is that of having to replace rotted posts. Also, set at least the corner posts and the gateposts in concrete and brace them well, the idea being to promote stability and durability.

Regardless of the type of fence you choose, prudence advises that you bury about twelve inches of rust-resistant, wire-mesh fencing in the ground near and extending several inches inside the fence line. Place the fencing at a depth of four inches and flat, at a right angle to the fence. The purpose, of course, is to prevent any dog from tunneling under the fence.

Exercise Yards

Do you plan to have a few? Provided they are escape-proof, such areas can be worthwhile additions to any boarding kennel. They afford pooch a chance to get off concrete for a while, and to run and stretch her legs while freeing her mind. Of course, escorting dogs to and from the yards takes additional time and effort, but the benefits to the animal's physical, mental and emotional well-being in terms of exercise, a break from the boredom of confinement and a measure of relative freedom are well worth it.

There are two problems attendant to the exercise-yard concept. First, soil cannot be as effectively disinfected as concrete. That is why dogs should be given run of a yard only after elimination. They may still mark areas of the yard, but that's dogs for you. Second, risk of injury or escape is greater. This is why yard time should not be allowed to diggers or fence climbers, suspected or confirmed. You may also wish not to grant yard time to a player—a dog who will not come when called, necessitating chasing the animal.

Landscaping and Decor

This section concerns your facility's appeal to your clients and to you. The dogs could care less that your property's lawns are well maintained, that you have flower beds or that the kennel building and the outside-run dividers are painted in an inviting, color-coordinated scheme. The idea behind creating an atmosphere that is as appealing to the owners as the kennel's comfort is to the dogs is to put people at ease. Because a nicely decorated kennel gives owners a sense of comfort and confidence about the care their pets receive, the owners— perhaps without any conscious intent or realization—transmit these feelings to their dogs, which are generally receptive to such messages. That makes it easier for a dog to accept being boarded (being away from family), which is a primary goal.

Another reason behind landscaping and decor is to provide you with a work environment in which you can take pride. To some folks, a career that frequently includes cleaning up dog droppings would be seen in the same light as a life sentence. You and I don't look at it that way, of course, and a facility whose appointments suggest a positive, feel-good-about-the-place attitude can help make sure that we never do.

In selecting colors for your kennel, avoid dark hues. They can lend a foreboding atmosphere to your building, and they do not reflect

A handy type of latch for exercise-yard gates. The latch snaps shut from the weight of the gate pushing against it. Note, too, that the latch can be locked, such as with a padlock.

A birdbath, a flower pot, and trees (not visible) can lend a homey quality to your kennels.

light well. However, don't go to the other extreme by selecting hospital white. We want to communicate sanitary conditions, yes, but not a message of cold sterility.

Sign

Like your choice of kennel name, the appearance of your kennel's sign can help you or hurt you. As it is likely the first expression of your business that a client will see, it is that person's first contact with your operation; it contributes to a customer's first impression of your facility.

Your sign should be professional in appearance. That is not to say that it has to be done by a professional sign painter. If you can do a good job of it yourself, there is no need to hire someone to make a sign for you. At the same time, if drawing and painting are not among your talents, you would be financially ahead contracting a professional's services instead of winding up with a sign that looks like I did it!

Avoid a specific breed shape or breed artwork for your sign, for the same reasons that it is unwise to include a specific breed as part of your kennel name. It is never shrewd to exclude by omission any segment of your potential clientele.

One final point: Should you have a sign at all? In most cases a sign identifying your business is worthwhile, but there are some instances in which a sign can actually be more of a problem than it is worth. My driveway, for example, begins at a considerable distance from my home and kennel. Placing a sign at the beginning of my driveway could easily lead to the sign winding up in some college student's dorm room. A second reason why I do not have a sign is because I do not want puppies to be dumped under the cattle guard separating my driveway from the county road. Some people do things like that.

Labor

In this chapter I have alluded more than once to the notion that in some phases of construction one may be able to perform the work oneself, the object being to reduce expense. Underscore the ''may'' in that observation, however; do-it-yourselfing is merely an option, not a recommendation. I know from personal experience that a person with decidedly limited construction skills can surprise him- or herself with what can come from a little research, some hard yet satisfying work and occasional coaching from construction professionals. The trick is to undertake only those jobs that one adequately understands and can physically handle safely. There are many risks in construction work, from power tools, ladders and materials, to enumerate but a few sources of potential disaster. There is also the danger that one might wind up spending more on error correction than would have been the case had professionals been contracted in the first place. Whether to involve oneself is largely a commonsense decision, and should be made in tandem with the notion that if you have the slightest doubt, stay with what you are good at, like dealing with man's best friend, and leave the building work to those who know how.

In hiring people to construct your kennel, it may be that you already know several professionals and know that they deliver on their promises: solid results at an agreed-upon price by the date specified. If you are shopping for help, however, investigate thoroughly all comers before committing yourself. Ask for a list of folks they have done work for and ask those people for their evaluations. A most revealing query can be ''Would you hire this person to do the same job again?'' Also, visit with building-material suppliers and ask for their impressions of the individual's work. Listen for what the suppliers do *not* say, be aware when issues are sidestepped and if you often hear a variation on "Oh, he's okay, I guess," keep looking.

A related concept in dealing with contract labor is that of "Get it in writing." Handshake contracts are all very well on the surface, but much grief can be avoided by obtaining written bids outlining the work to be done, the materials to be used, the total costs to you, when payments are due and the promised date of completion. Also, secure a waiver from anyone you hire, absolving you of any and all liability pertaining to on-the-job and related injuries from the beginning of the work until the date of the work's completion. Reinforce this caution by ascertaining that any contractor whom you engage carries his own health, accident and liability insurance. Don't just ask the contractor if he carries insurance: Get the name of his insurance agents and verify the facts with them.

Feline Facilities?

Here is an end-of-chapter thought in the form of a question: Do you intend to board cats as well as dogs? If you do, be sure to allow additional room for installation of a bank of cat cages, available from numerous suppliers. You will also need several more stainless-steel food and water bowls (as described in chapter 5, "Equipment and Supplies"), litter boxes and additional room for cat food and cat-litter storage.

Reflection

"Any place is good enough for a dog," is a venerable aphorism easy of quotation and capable of frequent application by those uninitiated in the management of dogs; but it is nevertheless wholly without foundation in fact, as those who have attempted to kennel valuable stock in unfitting quarters have discovered to their cost.
Vero Shaw, B.A.
The Illustrated Book of the Dog

4

Startup

KENNEL NAME

How important is the name you give your business? If you have good facilities and offer top-flight service at reasonable prices, does the name really matter all that much? You bet it does. Before RCA signed Elvis Presley to a recording contract, another major record company turned him down, an executive for the company saying that no one with a name like *that* would ever make it in show business. Granted, it was not the smartest thing that the record company ever did—the decision doubtless led to a great deal of finger pointing in the company's boardrooms over the years—but you get the idea: A wrong name for a business can not only blind people to its attributes, it can keep them from looking at it in the first place.

When choosing a name for your boarding kennel, there are four concepts to keep firmly in mind: *mass appeal, clarity, memorability* and *singleness of purpose*. A name like "Grannie Grump's Pooch Parlor and Storm Door Company" violates all four. Grannie may be the salt of the earth, as friendly, conscientious and caring a person as you would ever meet, but the image her name conjures suggests otherwise; it lacks mass appeal.

"Pooch Parlor" does not represent clarity in wording; the phrase may signify a boarding kennel but it could just as easily refer to a grooming salon (among other endeavors). The name itself is not only too long to be memorable, it features disparate concepts that obviously violate the singleness-of-purpose principle.

Mass appeal refers to choosing a name with which most people can feel comfortable. Your name and the word "kennels" might do the trick, especially if you are favorably known in your area as a dog person. A similar tack is to incorporate area themes into the business's name. At the same time, avoid regional references that have been overused. Several businesses where I live have already latched onto the *Cloud Peak* appellation. Thus, it is not a name I would consider were I establishing a kennel hereabouts. A related consideration is not using a name whose significance can change over time. "Edge-o'-Town Kennels" sounds fine today, but what if some years down the road your area grows and your location no longer is at the edge of town?

Preserve *clarity* by communicating the nature of your business through its name. The name "McGee's" might work in some instances, like a bar, a restaurant or a hair-styling salon, but a name like "McGee's Boarding Kennels" removes all doubt as to the nature of the business. "McGee's Pet Haven" might sound acceptable, until someone points out that "Pet Haven" could be suggestive of a pet cemetery, which is the last connotation to link with a well-run boarding kennel.

Obviously, the notion of using a *memorable* name refers to giving your kennel a name people can remember. Keep in mind that a short and simple name is usually preferable to one that is either long or complex.

Singleness of purpose is an edge you have over veterinarians who do boarding. Because boarding is not a sideline with you, say so in your kennel name. "McGee's Boarding Kennels" or "McGee's Dog Boarding" are examples of names that express singleness of purpose.

While not meaning to contradict myself, a name such as "McGee's Dog Boarding and Grooming" does not violate the singleness-of-purpose concept. Many dog owners view the two activities as so closely related as to be inseparable.

Breeders: Avoid linking the fact that you raise puppies (of any breed) with the name of your boarding operation. Doing so can suggest that your priorities are divided. Some folks might worry that the needs of their pets would be secondary to those of your pups. Also, consider how linking your boarding kennel name with that of a specific breed can have a negative effect. Let's say that you are a breeder of German

Shepherd Dogs. That's fine, but to name your facility ''McGee's German Shepherds and Boarding Kennel'' is to risk losing the small-dog crowd, as well as people who are intimidated by large dogs generally or German Shepherd Dogs specifically. Similarly, many large-dog owners spotting an ad for ''McGee's Toy Poodles and Boarding Kennels'' may keep looking. You and I know that a dog is a dog is a dog, but some owners of certain breeds would deem such a statement fallacious if not blasphemous. Unless you intend to house only certain breeds or sizes of *Canis familiaris*, be careful not to unintentionally limit your clientele.

Lastly, when choosing a name for your kennel, don't be susceptible to contracting a case of the cutes. A lady I know was going to name her facility ''The Flea Circus.'' Sure, it is a ''cute'' idea. You and I might get a chuckle out of it. But I have to wonder how many clients would be similarly amused.

RATES, FEES AND SERVICES

Structure

How much are you going to charge? Are you planning to offer different rates according to the sizes of the dogs? In a general sense, the first question has already been answered for you: If you are opening a new kennel, you would be ill-advised to charge more than established area rates. Your facilities may be nicer than those presently operating in your locale, but you are still the new kid on the block. To attract business you may have to appeal first to an owner's pocketbook. Your runs may be worth more than those of your competitors, but not to people who have never seen them, and if you start out charging more than established boarding operations, fewer folks will see them. If many area people are satisfied with your competitors, you have to offer something to get them to try your kennel. Lower rates is a quick way to get the ball rolling. You can always raise your fees once you have established yourself and have a solid, loyal following.

If you opt for a rate structure based on the size of the dog being boarded, do not make its composition too strict or too confusing. Keep it simple. A rate structure broken into too many categories can make some owners suspect that you are trying to get them. I charge one rate for any dog up to the approximate size of a Cocker Spaniel, and another rate for any dog larger than that.

Discounts

Let's say that a client wants to book space for an extended period, and asks if you would grant a discounted rate. First, what is an "extended period"? Some callers may feel that it is any period beyond a week, but I don't see it that way. To my view an extended period is a month or longer, and yes, I will reduce the daily rate for such a reservation. However, I advise the client that the discount applies only if the dog is with me for the total time reserved. If a person reserves a run for six weeks, for example, but returns after only three, the rate reverts to normal and the account is adjusted accordingly. I also tell the caller the terms for my discounted rates: "Half of the total amount is due when pooch arrives; the balance is payable when you return." This way I don't have so many dollars on the line if the person returns extremely early and tries to hold out for the discount anyway.

Now, a person has to use some common sense here. If a client books a run for eight weeks, and on that basis you grant a discounted rate, are you going to cancel the discount agreement if the individual returns five days early? I would not. Yes, I could, but doing so could well cost me future business from that client, and perhaps from his or her friends as well.

Another caller who may ask for a discount is the individual who feels she should get a break because she will be bringing the dog's food from home. As I point out to such folks, however, it is actually more work for me to have to keep track of who is being fed what than it is to feed all boarders the same food. The different foods also take up more space in my storeroom. For these reasons, I do not grant discounts to owners who bring their own vittles. To my knowledge, I have never lost a client over this policy.

A final discount-related question is: "Do you give your friends a break?" I do. "Even during your busier periods?" Yes. Though I can make a case for keeping business matters business, it is a personal choice with which I am comfortable.

Extra Charges

If a dog becomes ill and you have to take him to a vet, I suggest that you do not charge the client for your service. Sure, it says in the boarding contract that you can, but my experience is that such events happen so very rarely that it is better to settle for having the client's goodwill. When an owner asks, "What do I owe you for driving pooch to the vet?" an answer of "Forget it, I'm glad I could help" will do far more for your business long-term than a few short-term dollars ever could.

Some boarding kennel operators have told me that they charge additionally for dispensing medication. "It takes extra time, you know." Sure it does. At least a minute. Anyone who cannot give a pill, a liquid or ear or eye drops in that amount of time has not been in the business very long. Give pooch his pill or whatever and be grateful for the business.

Lightweight Grooming

Even if you do not offer total grooming services, related to the "Extra Charges" concept is the fact that you can offer basic grooming services without alienating the goodwill of local groomers. Clipping is out of the question, of course, but few groomers will be upset because you do bathing, brushing and nail clipping. Those are services that many people expect a boarding kennel to offer. Be sure to obtain the owner's written approval and release of liability for any sort of grooming, however. I know of one case where a dog's nail was accidentally clipped too short, the nail started to bleed after the owner took the animal home that day and the kennel operator was successfully sued for the services of a veterinarian and for the cost of having the owner's carpet professionally cleaned.

ADVERTISING AND PUBLIC RELATIONS

Types

Kennel operators often have to base their selection of the most advantageous advertising medium—radio, television or print—on cost: Few boarding kennels can afford to pop for TV ads. Determining the type of advertisement—splashy and ornate versus modest and unadorned—that will be most productive for your operation is often a function of locale: Certain advertising formats are more apropos in some regions than in others. However, there is one key to effective advertising: Constantly keeping your business's name in front of the public. True, it is wise to run test ads in various media occasionally, if for no other reason than to determine effectiveness. But you should have a core advertising program, even if it is only in the local newspapers and shoppers' guides classified sections, and those ads should be maintained year in and year out.

A Special Type

Especially in businesses such as boarding kennels and other dog-related activities (grooming, private training and training classes, for example), there is a second make-or-break form of advertising: word of mouth. Prime-time television advertising will not save a kennel that the public perceives as being dirty, poorly run and/or generally uncaring about its boarders. More than one client has told me, "My dog likes coming out here; she starts getting excited when we get within about a mile of the place." I know that people saying such things to me are communicating the same message to their friends, and that is not only a humbling compliment, it is the best form of advertising there is.

Less Obvious Forms of Advertising

You can greatly enhance your kennel's renown by participating in local dog-related activities, such as vaccination clinics, 4-H (or similar) dog projects and AKC fun matches. Not only can such ventures be enjoyable for their own sakes, taking part in community programs that pertain to dogs puts you more in the public eye and heightens your "dog person" status; it gets your name around.

"You send dogs *what*?"

A Christmas card is sent to every dog who has been boarded with me during the preceding two years. I address the envelope not to the owner but to the animal, as in "Buckwheat Jones." I started the practice partly out of sentiment—the holidays are for dogs, too, you know—and as a way of thanking the owners for their business. I did not realize at the time what a powerful impact it would have. As you know, many businesses send cards, calendars and the like during the holidays. The practice has become so routine that most people cannot remember which companies sent them cards last December. But very few folks will forget who sent their pet a holiday greeting, and as such it is a potent public-relations concept.

Reflection

Don't be afraid to take a big step if one is indicated. You can't cross a chasm in two small jumps.

David Lloyd George

5

Equipment and Supplies

THE LIST OF EQUIPMENT and supplies needed to effectively run a boarding facility is longer than many people might suspect. Of course, major equipment, such as heating and air-conditioning units, a hot-water heater, shelving, a telephone and a sink, are necessary for most boarding kennel operations, but they are not peculiar to the business. It is the list of distinctive-to-the-trade items that would surprise most folks.

Food- and Water-Related Supplies

Stainless-steel feeding bowls, in one-pint, one-quart and two-quart sizes, are unbreakable and are easy to clean. One of each size per run should provide an adequate inventory; using a permanent marker, number the bottom of each bowl for identification.

Galvanized or plastic garbage cans are useful for food storage, as they repel pests and moisture. It is helpful to label each can with the container's contents.

You will also need:

Plastic two-cup food scoops, one per food container

It's difficult to have too much shelving in a kennel.

Food bowls (and other supplies) arranged on shelves on which run numbers have been painted. Note the boxes on the upper shelf; also numbered to correspond with runs, customer equipment (leashes, collars, etc.) are kept in these containers.

Can opener

An assortment of spoons, forks and knives

Galvanized water buckets, one per run plus two extras, numbered with a permanent marker on the bottom for identification

Health Supplies

No boarding operation should be without a first-aid kit containing at least the following items:

A watch with a second hand

Adhesive tape (one-half inch, one inch and two-inch widths)

Alcohol

Blankets

Burn ointment

Cloth towels

Electric clippers

Electric heating pad

First-aid chart, such as the one that appears at the end of this book

Gauze pads

Hemostats

Hot-water bottle

Hydrogen peroxide

Ice-pack bag

Lengths of rope

Lengths of elastic

Merthiolate

Muzzles of varying sizes

Pen light

Quik-Stop (for halting minor bleeding, like from a broken nail or one that has been clipped too closely)

Rolled gauze

Razor blades (single-edged)

Scissors (straight, angled and blunt-edged)

Splint material

Stabilizing transport board with security straps and hand grips (like a stretcher, only solid; often made out of plywood and covered with canvas)

Syringes

Thermometers (2)

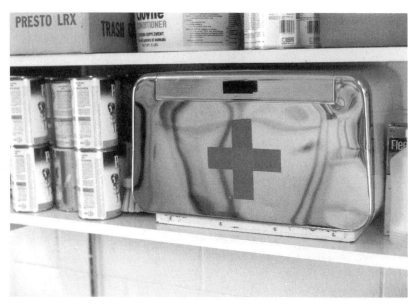

This breadbox makes an excellent container for first-aid supplies.

Tourniquet

Tweezers

Local veterinarians' telephone numbers

Two reference books (and more than a passing familiarity with their contents):

Dog Owner's Home Veterinary Handbook (Carlson and Giffin)

Medical & Genetic Aspects of Purebred Dogs (Clark and Stainer)

General health supplies, such as Pepto-Bismol and aspirin

Security/Emergency Equipment

Padlocks with which to secure runs and yard gates when you have to be away for a time. For simplicity, it is preferable that these padlocks be keyed alike.

Smoke alarms

Charged fire extinguishers

A list of emergency telephone numbers: veterinarians, your doctor, hospital, ambulance services, fire departments and law-enforcement agencies

Miscellaneous equipment, in this case an intercom that has been locked on so indoor kennel activity can be monitored from another location (such as the house), a smoke alarm, and ear protectors.

Grooming Supplies

This list will be considerably longer if you offer complete grooming services. Otherwise, the following essentials should be adequate:

Brushes
Combs
Grooming table
Hair dryer
Nail clippers
Rinses
Shampoos

Cleaning Supplies

This is a list of minimums. Some facilities will need additional supplies, such as a vacuum cleaner for indoor/outdoor carpeting.

Brooms
Buckets
Disinfectants

Two types of squeegees, the larger of the two—which is twenty-four inches wide—being more useful in outdoor runs.

Squeegees can be used for other than their intended purpose, such as latching a hard-to-reach window.

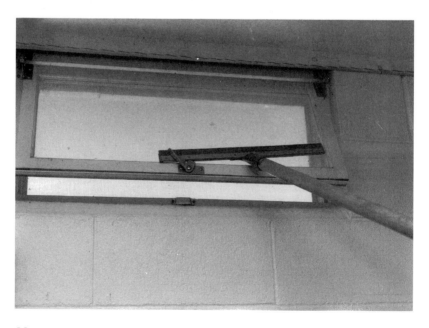

Feces scoops

Fly strips

Fly swatters

Hoses and nozzles—The hoses should be able to handle hot water without gradually disintegrating internally. However, do not use a hot-water hose for filling dog's water buckets, regardless of water temperature: Water of any temperature contacting the lining of a hot-water hose can produce a chemical reaction that can cause diarrhea.

Mops

Paper towels

Rubber kitchen gloves

Scrub brushes

Snow shovels

Soaps

Sponges

Spray bottles (plastic)

Squeegees

Wastebaskets

Window-glass cleaner

Maintenance Items

Like the Cleaning Supplies section above, this is a list of basic essentials. Your particular kennel may necessitate having additional equipment and supplies.

A spool of electric-fence wire (great for tightening or reattaching stretched chain-link)

Duct tape

Hammer

Heavy-duty wire cutters

Inside-drain plugs

Pliers

Plumber's helper

Plumber's snake

Screwdrivers (flat-blade and Phillips)

Tin snips

Miscellaneous Equipment

Given the needs of your particular operation, you may wish to add several items to this list, which is offered as a starting point.

Two flashlights, along with spare batteries and bulbs

Ladders that can safely reach your kennel's roof

Step ladders

Extra light bulbs

Adding machine

Pens and pencils

Notepad

Clock

Filing cabinet

Desk

Chair

Radio with an automatic shut-off feature, and set to a station offering restful music. Avoid screeching, God's-gonna-get-you preachers, heavy-rock music and debate programming, as such noises can make dogs nervous.

Blankets and terry-cloth towels for dogs to rest upon (but do not use these with dogs who tend to chew—ingestion of cloth can be fatal)

Leash-and-collar containers, one per run, numbered to correspond with each run, for storing owner's equipment

Regardless of whether you maintain an office in your kennel, you should have a telephone and something to write on in the building.

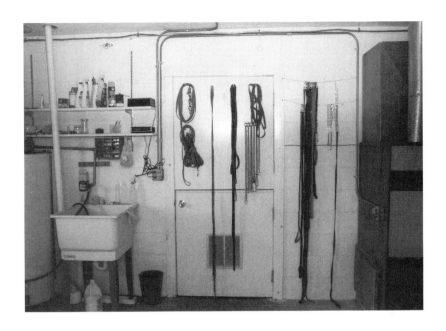

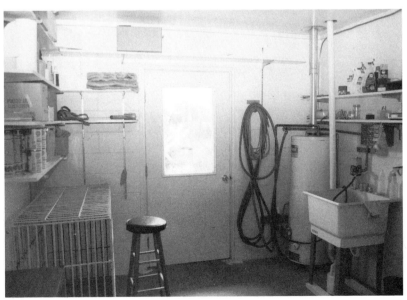

Two views of a kennel's storeroom.

Cages for housing destructive dogs
Welder's gloves for handling small, aggressive or fearful dogs
A noose-and-pole restraint
Small fan for circulating air
Large fan for drying runs
Room thermometers
Ear protectors (for you, not for the dogs)
Waterproof boots
Leashes and collars

Nightly Checklist

Prior to shutting down the kennel every night, review a written checklist to verify the following items:

All dogs inside?
Does each appear healthy?
Has all medication been dispensed?
Exterior doors locked?
Perimeter gates locked?
Each run access door closed?
Windows opened or closed, as needed?
Storeroom's interior door closed?
Food containers locked?
All water turned off at the source?
Radio set to switch off within half an hour?
Motion sensor on?
Intercom on?
Heat set for the right temperature?
Has everyone been petted today?
Has everyone had a good-night biscuit?

Suppliers

There is a number of reliable dog and kennel equipment suppliers currently operating throughout the United States and Canada. Most do a very brisk business in mail order, selling everything from rawhide and squeak toys to heavy-duty grooming and crating essentials. Generally speaking, their selections are admirably complete, their delivery prompt and their prices and service quite good.

In all likelihood, you are already familiar with several local and national suppliers from your other activities in dogs. Secure current copies of the various companies' catalogs for comparison purposes. Keep those catalogs close at hand: A kennel will have many needs and orders are usually rather frequent.

Experience will determine the companies you like best. You must be the best judge of how the different companies stack up to meet your needs.

Four-legged Wrecking Crews

Some dogs are incredibly destructive. I am not referring here to water-bucket spillers or blanket nibblers. Those are easy to deal with: Refill the bucket and remove the blanket. The destroyers I have in mind will often rip run-access doors from their tracks and make valiant attempts at chain-link destruction. While such animals are thankfully few and far between, housing them calls for extraordinary measures. Not only must you preserve and protect your kennel, you must protect the dog from itself.

While airline cages may successfully contain a destructive dog, I have seen large, powerful animals of this persuasion pop off a cage

A male German Shepherd created this damage to a run gate in less than ten minutes.

Three views of "The Cage," and its latching and locking systems.

door within minutes. Stainless-steel wire cages are equally ineffective. So what does one do?

My solution was to contract a local welding company to build an escape-proof cage. Measuring three feet high by two feet wide by four feet deep, the enclosure is constructed of one-half inch iron rebar spaced at two-inch intervals. My reaction upon seeing the finished product was that the dog who could escape from this cage would scare me half to death. A galvanized metal pan, which is removable to facilitate cleaning, lines the bottom of the pen to provide as much comfort as possible. Owing to its weight, the cage cannot be tipped over.

Regardless of how you plan to deal with destructive dogs, any boarding kennel should have at least one escape-proof, indestructible enclosure.

OPTIONAL EQUIPMENT

For Keeping Track of Who and What Is Where

You will need a dry-erase board and special-ink marker for recording dogs' names, the brand of food each is to be fed and how often and the food-bowl and water-bucket identification numbers. The board in my kennel is headed as follows:

Run#	Dog's Name	Food	AM	12	PM	Bowl	Water	Notes
1								
2								
3								

The headings and run numbers are inscribed using a permanent marker, while transitory information—dog's name, brand of food, amounts to feed, food-bowl and water-bucket numbers—is written with a pen containing a special ink that can be easily erased with a dry cloth. The headings *AM, 12* and *PM* refer to cups of kibble per feeding. *Bowl* and *Water* refer to the identification number for each container, the idea being to lessen the chance of inadvertently switching one

#	NAME	FOOD	AM	N	PM	DISH	H₂O	OTHER	L
1									
2	MOXEY	EM	1¼	-	1¼	16			
3									
4	PUPPY	EM	2	-	2	21			
5	HONEY & KISSES	EM	½	-	½	7			
6	TEDDY	own	½	-	½	6			
7	Brigette	EM	1½	-	1½	3			
8	DUDLEY	EM	2	-	2	14			
9	COCOA	EM	1	-	1	17			
10	ERIN-RAISADR	EM	1½	-	1½	20			

A board such as this can have many uses in a boarding kennel.

A 3-by-5 card attached to each interior run gate, reflecting the boarder's name and his veterinarian, provides essential information at a glance.

animal's food bowl or water bucket with another's. The *Notes* column is handy for recording medication frequency and dosages, and other uncommon information.

Yes, They're a Pain, However . . .

A telephone-answering machine can pay for itself by taking one call that you would have otherwise missed. Of course, an answering message should never be cold and unfriendly, but keep it brief, businesslike and to the point. A long message or one with idiotic sound effects will lose many a caller; a lot of people do not have the patience to sit through a rambling, infantile or hard-on-the-ears recording.

It's Not Really Equipment, but . . .

How about "Call Waiting"? This is a telephone-company service that informs you while you are on the phone that someone is trying to call you. There are advantages and disadvantages to the concept.

If your personal phone and business phone are the same, as is the case at many small-business operations, Call Waiting lets you know during another call that a client may be trying to reach you. At the same time, the service does not inform you who is waiting, just that someone is. The waiting caller may have even dialed a wrong number.

However, if you are talking with a client, Call Waiting can be a distractive nuisance. It is foolish to end a conversation with one customer simply so you can speak with another one. Also, the service is not free. Having it increases your costs of doing business.

In sum, my overall sense is that Call Waiting is a better deal for the phone company than it is for most kennel operations.

More About Telephones

Do you need a separate line for your kennel business, or is your home telephone adequate? Consider that telephone companies generally charge more for business service than for residential lines. If you have teenagers, or if there are other reasons why your home phone might often be busy, the increased monthly cost of a business phone might be money well spent: Customers do not like having to fight with a perpetual busy signal, and they may decide to solve the problem by calling someone else.

'Lightweight and easy to install, sun screens can markedly lower run temperatures.

The plastic material is easily attached to the outdoor run gate using electric-fence wire.

Miscellaneous Electronic Amenities

A motion sensor in the supply room, connected to an alarm in your home, is peace-of-mind equipment for detecting intruders or a dog who has managed to escape from an indoor run. Similarly, an intercom unit connected to a receiver in your house is most useful for monitoring routine kennel activity without disturbing the occupants.

Sun Shades

Depending on the amount of shade afforded by nearby trees, you may want to have a few rolls of sun-shade material for attaching across the tops and sides of your outdoor runs. Available in varying styles and colors, the material is lightweight, inexpensive, durable and easy to install. Do not leave sun shades attached during winter, however: The weight of accumulated snow—especially the wet, large-flake variety—can collapse your runs.

Run Guards

This plastic material is often used as kitchen-runner strip surfacing. Commonly available in one-foot widths, when attached horizontally to and flush with the top of a clean-out trough, the material prevents substances being hosed from the runs from splashing onto the walkway, deflecting them instead into the clean-out trough.

Reflection

Be prepared.
            Motto of the Boy Scouts of America

6

Comings and Goings

RESERVATIONS

New Clients

When a person with whom you have not done business before calls to reserve space, complete the following form:

Boarding Reservation

```
Caller:_____  Phone:_____
Date In:_____  Time:_____  Date Out:_____  Time:_____
Breed—#1:_____  Name:_____  Age/Sex:_____
Breed—#2:_____  Name:_____  Age/Sex:_____
Breed—#3:_____  Name:_____  Age/Sex:_____
Breed—#4:_____  Name:_____  Age/Sex:_____
Number of Dogs per Run:_____
Vaccinations:  □ Rabies      □ Distemper      □ Parvo-Virus
               □ Corona      □ Kennel Cough   □ Other:_____
Veterinarian:_____  Today's Date:_____
Notes:_____
```

The record's primary purpose is to document a starting point in your record keeping of a boarder's history. When taking reservations from established clients, since you already have most of the information on file, you need note only the person's name, arrival and departure dates and times and the date the reservation was received. In either case—with established clients or new ones—the next step is to allocate space for the reservation.

Reserving Space

Maintain monthly sheets having the following column and row headings:

Available Boarding Space

Month Of _____

Date	#1	#2	#3	#4	#5	#6	#7	→
1								→
2								→
3								→
4								→
5								→
6								→
7								→
8								→

With run numbers across the top and dates down the left side, this form serves the dual purpose of looking ahead and looking back. At a glance you can see which boarders are coming and going on any given date, as well as your run availability; the form is also useful for reviewing past business periods. Of course, more than one sheet per month may be necessary, depending on the number of runs at your facility.

Copy the client's last name from the *Boarding Reservation* form onto the line corresponding to the arrival date in any column. Allocate runs in numerical sequence whenever possible, using up the columns in left-to-right fashion; this makes it easier to see how much space is available for a given period. Unless your runs are of different sizes and appointments, it is not necessary to assign specific run numbers at this time. Recording a client's name under run number nine, for example, does not mean that his or her dog will occupy that exact run; we are accounting for the *number* of runs reserved for given dates, not for the specific runs.

Enter the planned arrival time in the upper-right corner of the block containing the caller's name; record the number of dogs per run in the block's upper-left corner. Line out the space the customer is reserving, writing the anticipated departure time in the upper-right corner of the last block needed. A sample entry follows for a client named Jones whose two dogs need one run, and who will arrive on the third of the month at nine in the morning, departing at six o'clock on the evening of the seventh.

Available Boarding Space

Month Of _____

Date	#1	#2	#3	#4	#5	#6	#7
1							
2							
3	²Jones⁹ᴬ						
4							
5							
6							
7	6P						
8							

Of course, in the happy event that a run will be used twice during the same day, either increase the size of the squares when preparing the form or plan on occasionally writing small.

For dogs who are being carried over into the next month, maintain continuity by drawing a down arrow (↓) in the client's column after the last day of the month, and enter the planned departure date below the arrow. Enter the names of clients whose pets are carryovers from the prior month on the first line of the new month's *Available Boarding Space* form, showing an up arrow (↑) for the arrival time.

After entering the necessary data on the *Available Boarding Space* form, file the *Boarding Reservation* form according to date of arrival.

Diagrammed

In terms of data flow, the reservation sequence is as follows:

The second step, "Complete *Boarding Reservation* form," can be skipped when dealing with established clientele. Because their pets have stayed with you before, information such as the dog's name, their veterinarian's name and so forth is already on file, and the requested arrival and departure dates and times can be entered directly onto the *Available Boarding Space* sheet.

ARRIVALS

On-Leash, Please

Insist that all dogs arrive (and depart) on-leash. Further, take pooch's leash from the owner as soon as they come through your main gate. In many states you are legally responsible for the animal from the moment he sets foot on your property, so it is prudent that you take control of his actions as quickly as you can. (It is wise to keep a few leashes and collars handy for instances when clients tell you, "I forgot my leash and collar at home.") Besides, landscaping is expensive, and you do not need for the animal to hoist a leg on a tree. The deed is not only rough on the tree, but of more importance is the fact that canine urine can be a transmitter of disease when a second dog sniffs the leavings of an afflicted animal.

Once you have control of the leash, close the main gate. Leashes and collars can break, and closing the gate lessens the potential for problems of flight. Then, if the dog is a first-time boarder, ask the owner to wait momentarily while you take pooch to his run. If the owner asks to accompany you to the area where his pet will be kept, honor the request.

Without Drawing Attention to the Fact . . .

Make a cursory examination of every dog upon arrival. Check for limping, hair loss, runny or glazed eyes, labored breathing or a persistent, dry, hacking cough. Should you observe any of these signals—or any others that you consider abnormal—stop right then and there and bring the matter to the owner's attention. Should the person be unable to explain the condition satisfactorily ("Yeah, he limps once in awhile; don't know why," "He always breathes hard in hot weather" and so forth), you may wish to refer the individual to a veterinarian before accepting the animal for boarding. You are not only within your rights to do so, you are trying to protect this dog as well as those who are already in your care.

Housing Assignments

Because dark-coated animals absorb more heat, house them on the side of your kennel that receives the least sunlight. Also, if one area of your facility is cooler than others, that is where to house the so-called Northern Lights breeds (Siberian Huskies, Alaskan Malamutes, Samoyeds and so on).

When you board dogs who are both playful and vocal, especially those from the same family, and you house them in separate runs, put some distance between them. This comes under the heading of maintaining a quiet kennel at night. If those dogs are housed so that they cannot see each other, they are less likely to be active. Granted, two dogs woofing at one another is not such a great problem, but the trouble is that their antics will likely set off the rest of the boarders.

To Avoid Problems

Place each new arrival in the outside section of his assigned run, keeping the door to the inside run closed for a few minutes to prevent the animal from entering his indoor run just then. The combination of travel and being in a new place often stimulates a dog to eliminate, and it is preferable that the animal sees from the onset that some things are better done outside than inside.

This Way You're Sure

There should be nothing in any run that a dog could catch his collar on. In deference to Murphy's Law, however, and the fact that a dog can catch a rear foot under a collar when scratching an itch about his neck, always remove each dog's collar. That way you can be certain an animal cannot catch its collar on anything.

Canine Comfort

If a dog seems nervous in his new surroundings, spend a few minutes with him after removing his collar. Pet the animal, talk to him, but keep your message an upbeat one of "I'm really glad you're here!" not "It's alright, don't worry" reassurance. Reassurance often deepens a nervous dog's anxiety, his reaction being, "If everything's so fine and dandy, then just what are *you* so concerned about?" Sure, spending several moments with the animal takes a little time. This may cause the owners to have to wait a few minutes until you return, but they'll keep. The dog's emotional well-being is your first concern.

Similarly, after you remove a dog's collar, should he trot away to check out his neighbors and investigate his new digs, leave the run without further ado. The critter is demonstrating that his mental and emotional states are fine, and that he wants to explore on his own. Your continued presence at this point can only complicate.

Good-bye, Hello

Another influence on a dog's mental state regards the owner. I have often seen people wave and call to their dogs as they depart, or when they arrive to collect their pets. Using the animal's name, they sing out their *auf wiedersehen*s or "We're backs."

The problem is that the message they are sending and the one the dog is receiving are two different things. In people terms, good-byes and hellos are ways of parting and greeting. In a canine's scheme of things, however, an owner calling to a confined animal from afar is teasing, pure and simple; it makes a dog nervous, anxious. A dog can have no earthly notion as to why his people have brought him to an alien place and left him there; he just knows he is there and that his family is not. Nor can the animal foresee that his owner will return for him. Of course, typical owners are unfamiliar with such concepts; they have never realized that a dog's perception of many events is different from that of a human's. But most will understand when you explain such things to them, and that will benefit everyone concerned: The owner will learn something about dogs, the animal will be more settled and you will not have to try to calm an upset dog.

Equipment Storage

Once you have left a new arrival in a run, place his leash and collar in an indoor container numbered to correspond with the run. This ensures that the owner will not inadvertently forget the equipment at home when he or she comes to pick up pooch.

Another line of thinking goes like this: Because an owner can arrive with pooch's collar so loose that the animal could pull his head out of it, some boarding kennel operators prefer to attach their own leash and collar, which fits more snugly, upon arrival. The owner's leash and collar is not kept at the kennel because the kennel operator also uses his or her own equipment during departures. That's all well and good, and I greet all arrivals with a large choker and leash in my pocket in case a dog's collar does appear loose, but I still prefer to retain the owner's equipment so I can be sure the individual will have a means for controlling the animal when they arrive home. True, in theory the dog is not my problem once he leaves my premises, but we all know the value of theories. By making certain that each owner arrives home with equipment for controlling his or her pet, I sleep better.

Boarding Record and Boarding Contract

After housing the dog, return to the owner and start a client/pet history by filling out the following *Boarding Record* form, being sure to record the equipment you are keeping and the date and time of arrival. In the event that the owner boards more than one dog with you, complete a *Boarding Record* form for each animal. True, much of the information is the same, but by having a record for each dog you avoid confusion when the owner subsequently does not board all of his or her pets with you, or when he or she no longer has one or more of the animals.

The next order of business is to secure the owner's signature on your *Boarding Contract*, a sample of which follows, and to provide him or her with a copy of the document if requested. In the case of an

Kennel Name

BOARDING CONTRACT

_____	_____
(Owner)	(Call Name)
_____	_____
(Address)	(Breed)

```
_____        at
(City, State, Zip)    _____  ___  ___  ___
                      (Age) (Date) (Sex) (Alt)

_____        _____
(Telephone)                (Veterinarian)
```

_____
(Medical Problems, Allergies, etc.)

Shots: Rabies   Distemper   Parvo   Corona   Kennel Cough

Food—Kennel's: _____   Amount per Feeding (Cups):
Food—Owner's: _____   AM_____   N_____   PM_____   E_____

IN Date/Time	OUT Date/Time	Clr	Lsh	Bed	Food	Med	Other	Charges

owner having several pets, you should have a separate signed contract for each animal.

Kennel Name

Address

City, State, Zip Code

BOARDING CONTRACT

This is a Contract between [Kennel Name] and the pet Owner.

Kennel agrees to exercise due and reasonable care, and to keep the kennel premises sanitary and properly enclosed.

The dog(s) is (are) to be fed properly and regularly, and to be housed in clean, safe quarters.

All dogs are boarded or are otherwise handled or cared for by Kennel staff without liability on Kennel's part for loss or damage from disease, theft, fire, death, escape, injury or harm to persons, other dogs or property by said dog(s), or for other unavoidable causes, due diligence and care having been exercised.

Owner agrees to pay to Kennel [rate, in numbers] ([rate, in words]) per pet per day for boarding service.

Owner understands and agrees that dog(s) picked up by Owner after 1:00 P.M. shall be charged for a full day's stay.

All charges incurred by Owner shall be payable upon pickup of pet(s).

Owner further agrees that pet(s) shall not leave the Kennel until all charges are paid to Kennel by Owner.

Kennel shall have, and is hereby granted, a lien on the pet(s) for any and all unpaid charges resulting from boarding pet(s) at Kennel.

If the pet(s) becomes ill or if the state of the animal's health otherwise requires professional attention, Kennel, in its sole discretion, may engage the services of a veterinarian of its choosing, or administer medicine, or give other requisite attention to the animal, and expenses thereof shall be paid by Owner.

It is understood by Kennel and Owner that all provisions of this Contract shall be binding upon both parties thereunto for this visit and for all subsequent visits. This Contract contains the entire agreement between the parties.

(Owner)	(Date)

(Kennel)	(Date)

As you see, the dog is not specifically identified by name, breed, or any other criteria in the *Boarding Contract*. This is because the document is printed on the reverse side of the *Boarding Record* form, making further identification of the animal unnecessary. The practice not only decreases by one half the number of pieces of paper you have to handle and file, it centralizes all data for each animal.

Also, notice that the dog is frequently referred to as a "pet." The idea behind such wording, instead of the more vague terminology "dog," is to lessen the odds of a massive lawsuit should a tragedy befall the animal while in your care, and the owner claims in court that the animal was a "show dog" of great value.

Boarding Record Continuation

Of course, the lines provided on the *Boarding Record* form for recording each visit will eventually be used up. At that time a continuation sheet, such as the sample below, will be needed.

Kennel Name

Boarding Record - Continuation Page #_

(Owner)	(Phone)	(Dog's Call Name)

IN Date/Time	OUT Date/Time	Clr	Lsh	Bed	Food	Med	Other	Charges

Computer Users

If your record-keeping system is on computer, the *Boarding Record* form can be modified and incorporated onto a single page with the *Boarding Contract*. As the sections for recording arrival and departure times, equipment and so forth can be entered into the computer, they can be eliminated from the *Boarding Record* form. The resulting modified *Boarding Contract* form appears as follows.

BOARDING CONTRACT

This is a Contract between [Kennel Name] and the pet Owner. Kennel agrees to exercise due and reasonable care, and to keep the kennel premises sanitary and properly enclosed. The dog(s) is (are) to be fed properly and regularly, and to be housed in clean, safe quarters. All dogs are boarded or are otherwise handled or cared for by Kennel staff without liability on Kennel's part for loss or damage from disease, theft, fire, death, escape, injury or harm to persons, other dogs or property by said dog(s), or for other unavoidable causes, due diligence and care having been exercised. Owner agrees to pay to Kennel [rate, in numbers] ([rate, in words]) per pet per day for boarding service. Owner understands and agrees that dog(s) picked up by Owner after 1:00 P.M.

shall be charged for a full day's stay. All charges incurred by Owner shall be payable upon pickup of pet(s). Owner further agrees that pet(s) shall not leave the Kennel until all charges are paid to Kennel by Owner. Kennel shall have, and is hereby granted, a lien on the pet(s) for any and all unpaid charges resulting from boarding pet(s) at Kennel. If the pet(s) becomes ill or if the state of the animal's health otherwise requires professional attention, Kennel, in its sole discretion, may engage the services of a veterinarian of its choosing, or administer medicine, or give other requisite attention to the animal, and the expenses thereof shall be paid by Owner. It is understood by Kennel and Owner that all provisions of this Contract shall be binding upon both parties thereunto for this visit and for all subsequent visits. This Contract contains the entire agreement between the parties.

(Owner)	(Date)

(Kennel)	(Date)

Also, if your system is computerized there is no need for a continuation form, of course, as there is when records are kept by hand.

Something for Pooch

After you have waved good-bye to the owners and they have departed, go spend a few minutes with their dog. Make a friend. The animal may be in something of a vulnerable state emotionally, having just watched his people leave, and it is a good time for you to take their place insofar as letting him know that you like him and can be trusted. This time is also an opportunity for you to get a reading on the animal's temperament and predispositions, which is information you need.

After visiting with the dog for a bit, open the animal's inside/outside run access door and place a bucket of cool, clean water in his indoor run. Make sure he sees you do this; he will likely view it as the act of a friend because it is reminiscent of something that his family does for him.* Placing the water bucket in the inside run also serves

---

*Should the dog appear to have aggressive or extreme territorial tendencies, however, you may want to protect yourself by placing the bucket in his indoor run prior to opening the inside/outside-run access door, or at a time when he is outside and near the outside-run gate.

to designate that area as "home" or "the nest," suggesting by implication that it is not to be fouled. A fresh capful of the product *ReaLemon* added to a dog's drinking water, by the way, can be very effective in decreasing the odds that the animal will develop an intestinal upset caused by differences between the water chemistry at his house and your kennel.

"Who Dat?"

Near the top of each inside-run gate is a clip into which I insert a three-by-five card that states the dog's name, the owner's name and the name of his or her regular veterinarian. The information is not only helpful to me in getting to know new boarders, it saves time looking up details should an emergency arise.

DEPARTURES

Check-Out Time

As you may know, hotels charge for a full day if a guest has not checked out by a certain hour. Given the conceptual similarities between hotels and boarding kennels, I follow the same principle, my check-out time being 1:00 P.M.

Some clients think twenty-four hours should be a day in boarding terms, and in their place, you and I might see it similarly. That is why I explain to those who question the policy: "Many folks drop their dogs off in the morning, and if I let animals stay much past the lunch hour at no charge, it is likely that I will have to turn down another client to do so, thereby losing that day's revenue on a run." Most come to see and understand my position.

Now, does this mean I will zing customers for a full day's boarding should they pick up their dog at 1:08 in the afternoon? Of course not. If we are referring to a frequent boarder, I would even stretch the check-out time by an hour or so as long as I do not have to turn away business to do so. What if it is the slow time of year, and the client, whose dogs have been with you for three weeks, shows up at 2:20? Do you assess another day's boarding? I would not, but I would make sure the owners know that they are getting a break. "Check-out time is one o'clock, but we'll skip that today" is a friendly way of stating your case.

Settle Account First

A small point of procedure pertains to settling the account, specifically "When?" When a client arrives to pick up his or her best friend, I report the amount due and ask the owner to prepare a check while I go get pooch. To first-time boarders I explain, "It's just easier to get the paperwork out of the way before you and your pal are reunited. This way you can give your dog your full attention when I return with him."

Cash or Charge?

I accept local checks or cash. Whether you should add credit cards to your list is a decision only you can make. I do not take plastic for the simple reason that it is too time-consuming for me, and doing so would add to my costs of doing business. To my knowledge I have never lost a client over the issue. Very few folks have ever even broached the question.

A related consideration is whether to establish personal charge accounts. I have always operated my kennels on a "cash-and-carry" basis, explaining to the few who have asked about charging that I do not want to get into the extra bookkeeping that charge accounts necessitate. Again, I have yet to lose any business because of this policy.

Receipts

Though several types and styles of receipt blanks are commercially available, you can lessen the expense by creating and duplicating your own. Receipts should be sequentially numbered, and should reflect the client's name, the date of payment, the amount of the transaction in numbers and in written form, what the payment is for (i.e., "Boarding—Old Buster") and the signature of the person receiving the payment. A sample receipt form appears on page 114.

113

```
                        Kennel Name

                 Receipt #_____

Received From _____    Date _____

Amount _____ Dollars


    ┌──────────────────┬──────────┐
    │ Account Total    │ $        │     Payment For _____
    ├──────────────────┼──────────┤
    │ Paid This Date   │ $        │     _____
    ├──────────────────┼──────────┤
    │ Balance Due      │ $        │     Received By _____
    └──────────────────┴──────────┘
```

Reflection

I'm really innocent—I only look guilty.

Caption on a poster depicting a
worried-looking Dachshund puppy

7

Policies, Practices and Direction

CLIENT ISSUES

Don't Sublet

Let's say that it is one of those joyous times when your kennel is booked to overflowing. A valued client calls, asking if you have space for Old Buster. You don't, but you know that Old B. is a most gentle animal and that another boarder whose disposition is very similar is already in house. Your impression of both dogs is that they would not fight for any reason. Do you allow them to share a run?

No.

Let's make it trickier. Let's stipulate that Old Buster's owners and those of the other dog—we'll call him Clyde—are next-door neighbors, and Old B. and Clyde are littermates who have often played together since they were pups. Now, given those circumstances, do you allow them to share a run?

No.

What if the caller points out, "Look, I know Clyde is there with you. He and Old Buster get along very well. How about putting them in together? It's certainly okay by me."

No. Not without the permission—and here's the key—of *both* owners. To put any animal in with Clyde without his owner's consent—or to put one animal in the inside portion of the run and another in the outside section, while keeping the run access door closed, effectually separating the dogs—is not only morally and ethically wrong, it violates stipulations contained in the boarding contract, specifically those phrases that read, "due and reasonable care," "the dog is to be . . . housed in . . . safe quarters" and "due diligence and care having been exercised."

Perhaps an operator might think to him- or herself, "So, what about sticking that Pom in number six in an airline cage for a few days? I could take Old Buster that way." Sure, that would work, but I recommend against it. The Pom's owner is paying for a run, not a cage, and while I have no problem with caging a dog for a short time (like for a half hour or so) until another dog is picked up, thereby freeing a run, it is wrong to meaningfully deprive an animal of proper housing simply to sweeten the day's take.

Is there any way Old Buster's owner can be accommodated? That depends on whether another dog will be leaving soon. If so, I would be willing to simply keep Old B. in my house until a run opens, and have done so on more than one occasion for valued customers. During a particularly hectic Christmas some years ago, in fact, one client's German Shepherd Dog was given free run of my house and slept on my bed for three nights until a kennel run became available. (The only problem then was that the animal didn't think much of going into a run later.) The point is, however, that there is often an ethical way to accommodate most customers during peak times without shortchanging other boarders in the process.

Having Said All That . . .

I would allow Old Buster and Clyde to play together, under supervision, in the same exercise yard provided that both owners approve the practice. If either owner is uncomfortable with the idea, I do not allow the dogs to be together for any reason.

Intentional Overbooking

Some kennels deliberately take more reservations than they can handle, their intention being to cover themselves against having unoccupied runs as a result of clients not arriving as scheduled and last-minute reservation cancellations. The number of runs by which such businesses overbook is commonly determined by seasonal factors and a percentage formula. While the idea may have merit at very large operations, it is a fool's game for a relatively small kennel. The question becomes not *will* you eventually have a problem of more dogs than runs, but *when* will you have a problem of more dogs than runs.

Strange Ways

Over the years a few callers have informed me that their dogs had not and would not receive any of the traditional vaccinations because they—the callers—did not believe in the concept of preventative medicine. I declined to accept their business, a policy that I suggest you follow as well. To do otherwise is to court potential professional disaster by endangering your other boarders. Any dog you board should be currently vaccinated against Distemper, Leptospirosis, Hepatitis, Parvo, Rabies, Corona and Tracheobronchitis (Kennel Cough). If you have any doubts as to a client's veracity, you are well within your rights to ask for a written certification signed by a veterinarian, attesting that the animal is current on all shots.

There have also been callers who wanted to bring their pets to the kennel as early as five o'clock in the morning. After pointing out that my hours for accepting and releasing dogs are from seven in the morning until ten at night, seven days a week, most were content to bring their animals at a more reasonable hour. A minority made arrangements elsewhere, which was probably just as well.

Understand, I have taken dogs at all hours when clients have been faced with an emergency situation. That is an obligation I feel toward any customer. But to routinely accept reservations for arrival before the roosters rise not only upsets the patterns of the dogs currently boarded, it makes for too long a day.

Incidentally, the policy of releasing pets as late as ten o'clock at night provides a significant edge on the competition. When people return from a trip they want their dogs, and while folks will abide a policy of "We close at five," they don't like it. They put up with it because they have no choice. The problem is compounded when the owners have to work the day after their return, and—because they cannot get their pooches until after work—are charged for another day's boarding. By making late pickups available, a kennel increases its goodwill.

Sshhh

It may happen that a caller will ask, "Are you boarding the Smiths' dog right now?" The answer to that question is a variation on "I'm sorry, but I can't give out that information."

Sure, in most cases the question's basis is innocence, but it may happen that the caller has evil doings in mind, such as burglarizing the Smith residence, and is trying to verify that the Smiths are indeed away for a time.

A similar situation can go like this:

"I'm here to pick up the Smiths' dog."

"Who are you?"

"I'm John Jones, the Smiths' neighbor."

"I'm sorry, Mr. Jones, but if the Smiths' dog is indeed here I can release the animal only to the owner. It has to do with protecting clients and their pets and maintaining confidentiality, don't you see?"

Again, it may well be that there is no problem here. Perhaps the individual is who he says he is, and it could be that the Smiths did contact him and request that he collect their dog. However, unless the client has made such arrangements with you in advance, you are putting yourself at risk legally by acknowledging that the dog is at your facility, and that risk is compounded if you release the dog to anyone other than the owner without the owner's authorization.

A Question to Ask

Make a point of asking clients—especially new ones—"Will you be coming after your pet yourself?" If a spouse will be picking up the animal, advise your client that the individual must bring identification in order for you to release the dog.

Who Needs the Aggravation?

Keeping a list, mentally at least, of your better clients is probably a suggestion nobody needs. It is only common sense to do so. But how about a roster of those people whose business you are better off without? For purposes of organization, my *No-No* list has three categories: No-shows, bad checks and chronic complainers.

No-shows are folks who honor about half the reservations they make, who not only fail to arrive, but who never call to let you know that they are not coming. *Bad checks* are self-explanatory. An individual who writes me a single "NSF" (non-sufficient funds) instrument does not get put on this list—accidents can happen—a second rubber check, however, constitutes automatic induction to my hall of infamy. The *chronic complainers* are the smallest group and are characterized by the fact that nothing pleases them. Understand, if a client has a criticism or a complaint, I want to know about it. Customers can see things that you and I might miss—our closeness to the operation can distort our perspective—and I appreciate it when a person takes the time to point out something that they think could be improved. Habitual whiners are another story. They gripe when they get here, again when they collect their pet and probably during their entire trip. I have been fortunate to have had only a small number of such contacts over the years, and in each case my runs were all taken when they called again for reservations, if you take my meaning. I follow the same policy with no-shows and bad-check writers. All three groups represent grief no boarding kennel needs.

Premature Departures

A situation you will have to face pertains to clients who return earlier than planned. They book a run for a week, for example, but arrive to pick up pooch after five days. Question: Do you charge them for the time they reserved—seven days—or for the five days that they actually used? Or, do you split the difference at six days rental?

My policy has always been to charge clients for time used, irrespective of what was booked. There have been a few good people who offered to pay for the time reserved, but I have yet to accept their kind offers. My reasoning is twofold. First, I am not comfortable with the notion of collecting a fee for something I have not done. Second, I want to hear from the client again. We all know what it is like to be "nickeled and dimed," and you know as well as I that such experiences left us with a bad taste and a resolve to shop elsewhere next time. Boarding kennel clients are no different. Trying to collect for time unused only incurs bad will.

Kennel Inspections by Clients

Why not? Every so often a caller will ask to look over my facility prior to making a reservation, and I am happy to oblige and to answer any and all questions. However, I do request that callers let me know when they will arrive so I can schedule time for them, and that they not bring their dog with them. A strange dog wandering about the kennel is too upsetting to the boarders in house.

DOG ISSUES

Cover Thine, and the Dog's

In *Dog Logic—Companion Obedience*, I wrote, "Don't acquire a canine you can't easily control physically in any situation when the animal is full grown." The same principle applies to boarding-kennel operators in the sense that they should not take any dog they cannot handle physically in a high-stress situation. To do otherwise is to put oneself at risk with large, aggressive dogs. Sure, everything would probably be okay, but if a problem did develop you could find yourself in a world of hurt.

Also, to board more dog than you can handle is to possibly endanger the dog. How? Let's say you have an emergency requiring immediate veterinary attention—you *must* get a boarder to a vet right away. Now let's make that dog about 180 pounds' worth of unconscious Saint Bernard. Can you get that much deadweight to and into your vehicle? What if the animal were conscious but delirious—could you control him sufficiently to get him to a vet? If the answer to either question is no, should you board an animal of such size and weight in the first place? The answer to that question is also no. That is what I mean about possible endangerment, unintentional though it might be.

Females in Season

The question is whether to board them; my policy is not to. Sure, there is a host of sprays and such on the market to knock down the odor, but the canine nose is keen, and chemical masks are only so effective in deceiving other animals. They soon learn that a lustful lady is in the area and the incidence of fence fighting becomes greater and more intense. In short, the charged atmosphere inflicts too much stress on everyone, including the female.

"You Know, That Dog Ain't Acting Right"

I tell owners who ask, "About all a dog has to do is look at me cross-eyed and I'm taking her to a vet." Seriously, I have to see a bit more symptomatology than that before bundling a dog off to the good doctor, but not too much more. Remember: I am not a veterinarian. Of equal importance are the facts that I am not familiar with every aspect of each boarder's medical history, nor do I consider myself an expert on every health nuance peculiar to every breed. The guidelines I follow are twofold and simple:

1. What would I want a kennel operator to do if it were my dog in question?
2. If in doubt, call a vet.

I would much rather run up a client's vet bill unnecessarily than risk his or her pet's health.

Infirmary

A related question is whether to maintain isolation runs for sick animals. My thoughts are that the veterinarians already have such facilities, and that the last thing my other boarders need is exposure to contagious diseases. Ergo, I do not have an infirmary.

Respite

When engaged in what I call "puttering-around" work in the kennel, I often let one of the dogs out to run around inside the building. I do not do this when working with powerful cleaners and the like; that could put pooch at risk. Nor will I let out a dog who I sense would tend to go from run gate to run gate, seeing what kind of trouble she could stir up. But with friendly dogs whom I have come to know over time, dogs who appreciate the chance for human contact, why not? It gives them a break from boredom, makes them feel special, and I enjoy the company.

"Well, If You'll Do That . . ."

What about bringing a boarder into your home for a few hours at a time? My answer is a second question: "Why not?" Many of the dogs you board are house pets, and allowing those whom you feel you can trust to visit with you *en casa* is a fringe benefit, for your clients and for their pets—and for you.

It Is Inevitable

Someday a dog will die while in your care. That's a harsh statement but it reflects a reality of the business. I have been fortunate that—even given the number of years I have operated my kennel and the number of dogs that have stayed with me—I have yet to have it happen. Thus, I cannot tell you from personal experience what to do, but I can tell you what I intend to do should the grim reaper arrive to claim a client's pet while boarded.

When I take an older dog, or one who has a history of serious medical problems, I have a talk with the owner. "Look, we both know that Fritzy is getting on in years (or, has not been well). In cases like this I have to know the owner's preference should the animal's time come while in my care." My question, of course, is what the owner would like done with the body. Though some callous souls have told me to "Take her to the landfill," most have asked that I take their pet to their veterinarian.

Not incidentally, in such an unhappy circumstance should the owner be charged a transporting fee? Of course not. If anything, send the owner a sympathy card.

FEEDING

Kibble Storage

Dry food is best stored in metal or plastic trash cans, appropriately labeled with the contents. (Labeling, incidentally, should be on the containers themselves, not on the lids—lids can get switched.) Such cans are easily obtainable, inexpensive, and they preserve freshness by repelling pests and retarding moisture. The containers should be of the locking variety to prevent invasion by a dog who has managed to escape from her run. True, the runs are designed to be escape-proof, but be assured that canine Houdinis *do* exist. Over the years I have met a few who possessed astounding escape abilities. Also, it is possible to forget to lock a run. That should never happen, I grant you, but Murphy's Law operating in conjunction with human fallibility makes the potential for error a strong possibility. Should an unattended dog get into the storeroom by any means, the practice of keeping food in locked containers certainly raises the odds that the animal will not be able to invade the food supply. Incidentally, you might want to look into the fact that there are dog-food companies who will provide you with storage containers if you use their products.

A lesser-known aspect of kibble storage is that more than one major dog-food maker recommends against storing their product in any container other than the packaging in which it is sold. Plastic contain-

Be sure to place the entire food sack into the container.

ers, they claim, and the tin element present in metal ones can draw out and otherwise damage nutrients from kibble that comes in contact with the container, greatly reducing the food's nutritional value. I have little formal knowledge about chemistry but sense that these claims may be valid, and in any case there is no reason to dispute the recommendation. I still store the food in locking containers, for the reasons stated above, but I do not empty the food bags into the cans; I place the entire sacks in the containers. At feeding times, after scooping out the amounts needed, I fold the surplus packaging over the food to close the sack. Kibble manufacturing representatives assure me that this method of storage ensures that their products will retain their nutritional value, as the food is never in contact with the container.

Meal Time

Though very young dogs may require a noon meal, it is best to feed boarders twice daily: early morning and evening. This is preferable to a single daily feeding for several reasons, the most important of which is that in many breeds a massive ingestion of protein can trigger

123

the onset of *torsion* (more commonly known as bloat), which can easily be fatal. The twice-daily feeding schedule also increases the number of pleasant events the boarders have to look forward to. Too, it facilitates run cleaning in that it tends to cause most of the dogs to eliminate within minutes of each other, rather than throughout the day.

The policy of feeding boarders twice daily also makes for a quieter kennel. Following occasional post-meal friskiness by younger animals, most canines tend to settle down and snooze following a meal. This tendency is especially noticeable after the evening meal, which should be presented around sundown; that is when dogs naturally eat. In any case, do not feed during the hottest part of the day. Doing so can cause a dog to regurgitate.

Some owners will tell you that they leave their dog's food bowl down throughout the day (known as on-demand feeding), and I have found that it is best to observe the owner's practices whenever possible. This is especially important with older boarders: There is no point in further upsetting the routine of an aged animal who is set and secure in her ways. Being separated from her people is stressful enough. Even with younger dogs, however, I do not leave food bowls in the runs after the evening feeding, regardless of the owner's feeding practices. This is simply because a dog who has access to food at all hours is likely to foul her indoor run, and possibly her sleep blanket and herself, during the night, which can make for an ungodly mess by morning. It is also upsetting to other boarders to hear a neighbor enjoying a two-in-the-morning snack, and realizing that they have nothing for themselves.

A subtle yet significant aspect of feeding technique is to bring all the readied food bowls into the inside run area of the kennel before giving anyone their food. This allows each dog to receive her meal within seconds of her neighbor, instead of having to wait while the kennel operator treks to the storeroom to carry what bowls he or she is able, feed a few dogs and repeat the process. It can make a dog anxious to have to wait several minutes for her food to arrive when she can hear others eating. The practice of bringing all the bowls to the kennel room before handing out the first meal causes a minimal amount of time to lapse between feeding the first dog and the last one.

When two dogs occupy the same run, it is often necessary to feed one of them outside and the other inside. Most owners who board more than one dog in the same run will tell you if their dogs should be fed separately, but don't count on it. Also, dogs who peacefully eat side by side at home may react differently in a boarding situation. If you have any doubts, split the animals for the short time it takes them to eat.

Allow about ten minutes for each dog to consume her meal. I would never advise removing a dog's food bowl while the animal is in mid-bite simply because an arbitrary number of minutes have passed. That would not only be unfair to a slow eater, it might result in being snapped at. But when ten minutes have lapsed, or when it is apparent that a dog has either finished eating or has lost interest in her meal, remove the bowl. Wash the emptied ones, and cover those still containing food, refrigerating them if necessary.

This is also a good time to check everyone's water, cleaning and refilling those buckets that need attention. You will be cleaning runs in a few minutes, and can then turn your attentions to other matters while the dogs settle for a time.

Cost of Dog Food

There are two ways to accumulate money. First, earn it; second, hang on to as much of what you have earned as possible. A major expense of operating a boarding kennel is food. The question, then, is how to keep that cost low. There are two methods. One, use cheap food. Knowing that you get what you pay for, that method is unacceptable. Many of the so-called bargain brands are of a quality and nutritional level that a dog would be as well off eating garbage. I offer my

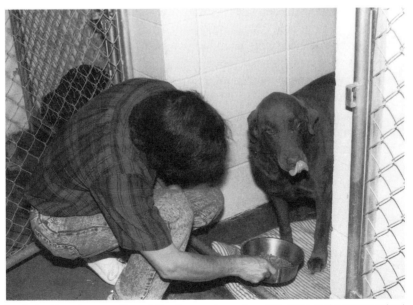

Don't do this unless you "know" the dog—put your face this close to the wrong animal and you may need stitches.

boarders the same food my dogs eat, and to my mind it is the best kibble available. So how does one provide quality food at low cost?

First, buy in quantity. Speak with the manufacturer—*not* with the supplier—and find out two things: the product's shelf life, and its age when shipped to your supplier. Then determine how much food you can use during a time period that does not come close to exceeding the shelf life limit or overtaxing your storage facilities. Make your supplier aware that you always want food from incoming shipments, not bags that have sat in a warehouse since the last shipment.

Second, make the best deal on price that you can with your supplier. Emphasize that you will promote the product by telling every client the brand of food you are using and where you purchase it, that you feed it to your own dogs and that you will offer clients take-home samples (at the supplier's expense, of course).

A Bedtime Snack

Every night, just before you shut down the kennel, give each boarder a dog biscuit, saying each dog's name as you present the animal with the treat. Yes, this raises your dog-food cost by a few bucks a week, but the rewards are worth the additional minor expense.

Besides, the cost can be kept low by using store-brand generics. The nutritional worth of the snack is of no real import anyway. Nutrition is what dog food is for. The value of a nightly biscuit is that each animal receives a little extra attention. For just a moment pooch has contact with a human. She hears her name and is handed a morsel. It is a pleasant moment for her, both in terms of sensation and emotion. It is caring, and dogs know a lot about that.

Not incidentally, do *hand* that dog her biscuit; do not just toss it into the run. You will not be bitten as long as you keep your fingers outside the chain-link. If a dog goes for the treat in too aggressive a fashion, quickly pull it back a few inches, make eye contact (the dog will look questioningly at your eyes when you withdraw the biscuit), calmly and gently tell her "Easy" (the technique of stretching the word out a bit aids communication) and slowly offer it to her again. After one or two tries that leave the dog coming up empty, she will get the word and soften her approach.

In a sense, the pre-sleep tidbit makes for a quiet kennel at night. The animals learn that the snack is, as I said, something that precedes sleep. In that context the biscuit has a mild sedating effect. (A friend who is a computer addict but who is not a dog person once commented,

"I fail to see how a biscuit having no sleep-inducing chemical properties can affect an animal like that." I asked my friend if he had ever heard of Pavlov, he asked if that was a computer language and the discussion sort of fizzled out.) As I imagine you may have surmised, it is not so much the biscuit that causes the dogs to settle, it is the ritual and its effect on an animal whose behaviors are extremely patterned by nature.

CLEANING AND DISINFECTING

How Often?

Good times to clean and disinfect all runs are shortly after the morning and evening feedings, especially the morning one. The runs, which may have been spotless prior to feeding, will in all probability be anything but shortly thereafter. Of course, any run should be cleaned and disinfected between occupants, as any run should be cleaned and disinfected as the need occurs.

While you are cleaning outside runs, dogs occupying those runs should be kept in their inside runs, and vice versa. No dog should ever be allowed to traipse through disinfectants or cleaning solutions. To declare that such chemicals can be hazardous to a dog's well-being is to grossly understate the danger: Ingestion of some cleaning and disinfectant agents can easily be fatal. Of course, if you are only using water to do quickly hose down a run, there is no need to lock up pooch. She may enjoy watching what you are doing, and if she stands next to you while you are working, it gives you an opportunity to check your coordination: hosing with one hand while petting the dog with the other.

With What?

Runs should be cleaned and disinfected using whatever compounds and products your veterinarian recommends. Not only are there geographical differences vis-à-vis the necessity to guard against certain diseases and parasites, for me to recommend specific brand names is to risk legal entanglements. Moreover, because germ resistance levels to cleaners and disinfectants can and do change, the best advice I can offer in good faith about what chemicals to use for sanitizing your runs is "Check with your vet."

An easy way to keep snow from sealing outdoor drains.

Flies and Other Bugs

In case no one ever told you that flies and other insects come with operating a boarding kennel, they do. The problem is how to deal with the cussed little buzzers. Chemical sprays are out of the question as they are potentially harmful to dogs as well as to bugs. Electric fly-zapper lights are fine, except they are expensive to operate and they leave one to wonder if they don't just attract insects from greater distances, insects that might not have visited your premises otherwise.

The best product I have found for controlling winged pests are the old-fashioned fly strips that a user unrolls and hangs from the ceiling. The bugs are attracted by the strip's odor, but upon landing they discover that the strip is also extremely sticky, so much so that they are unable to depart. The drawback to fly strips is that they are unsightly, especially when festooned with uncountable winged annoyances. Such a coating demonstrates how well the strips work, however, and they do so at no danger to any boarders. Fly swatters are also effective, but anyone who operates a kennel is usually too busy to wield a fly swatter.

Whenever you enter an outside run without first putting the boarder inside, lock yourself into that run. Exception: If you are dealing with a dog on the fight, you may need to make a hurried exit.

The person who can't find time to spend a few minutes with boarders is in the wrong business.

Look Out Below!

If you plan to top your outdoor runs with some form of wire-mesh fencing, as recommended, and if you live in the snowbelt, be prepared to clear snow from those tops, even during a raging blizzard. Wet, large-flake snowfall can rapidly seal the run tops—even those covered by widely spaced mesh—with a deep blanket of sufficient weight as to bend the supporting side panels, including those made of chain-link. A quick, safe and easy way of clearing the overhead fencing is to enter an outdoor run (having first put its occupant inside), and swat the underside of the mesh with the flat side of a broom. The snow falls through the fencing to the run's surface, you sweep out as much as you care to and—while giving thanks that you had the foresight to wear a heavy, water-repellent, hooded coat—go to the next run and repeat the process.

Also During Winter

Invert a bucket over each of your outside drains during a snowfall. This practice helps prevent snow from accumulating in a drain to the point of sealing it, which can force escaping septic gases into your kennel building.

GENERAL

"Hello There!"

Whenever you walk through or by your kennel, say each current boarder's name at least once. It is a small matter, true, but only to you and me. To the dogs it is an event, and a pleasant one at that.

Keys

Keep all kennel keys, including those to padlocks, on the same key ring. Use a short length of lightweight chain to attach the key ring to a wooden paddle or the like to lessen the chance of misplacing it. Whenever possible, key alike as many doors and padlocks as you can.

Plan Ahead

Periodically inspect your kennel from top to bottom, noting on a sheet of paper those matters that need repair or improvement. Then, when you experience a slow period, you can have your supplies and equipment already on hand and you will be ready to take care of the problems you have unearthed.

No Smoking Allowed

Discourage smokers from pursuing their habit in your kennel building. They may tell you that their pets are accustomed to it, but the point is that other boarders may not be. Dogs avoid tobacco smoke whenever possible (thereby demonstrating—at least in the case of owners who smoke—a better fix on reality than their "masters"). Dogs in your care should not be subjected to the harsh smell of tobacco and its potentially harmful effects.

Pickup and Delivery

After writing this section's title I jotted down two words: "whether" and "insurance." Whether to offer the service of pickup and delivery and the need for insurance to cover such trips. The decision to offer pickup and delivery is one that only you can make. Factors relating to the decision are regional competitors' practices, the time involved and the need for such a service in your locale. I do not offer the service per se, though I have been known to pick up or deliver someone's pet under unusual circumstances.

Insurance

The best advice I can offer on the subject of insurance for any phase of your business is to remember that ours is a lawsuit-happy society, and that you should have a word with your attorney and with your insurance agent. You might also look into policies offered through industry associations. My thought is not to skirt the insurance issue; I choose to avoid it altogether. My motivation is twofold: fairness toward you—I am a dog trainer and kennel operator, not an insurance expert— and the fact that I have yet to comprehend any insurance policy's fine print. There are just too many ifs, ands, buts, maybes and not-if-we-don't-have-tos in the insurance game for an amateur player like myself to advise someone else how to proceed.

Inc.?

A related consideration is incorporating your business so that in the event of a lawsuit, you—as an individual—would be more protected than you might be otherwise. I cannot tell you whether incorporation would be the right move for you; I can only mention it as an option. My suggestion is that if the idea has appeal, visit with an attorney about the advantages and disadvantages of incorporating your business.

Licenses

In your local area, do boarding kennel operations have to be licensed? Are there business taxes you have to pay? Is a boarding kennel subject to the whims of regulatory agencies where you live? As the answers to these and similar questions vary from region to region, the best advice I can offer is that you explore these questions and related concerns with your attorney.

Kennel Helpers

Finding, screening and training kennel personnel is an art form. Even before looking for a helper, though, one should acknowledge the fact that some folks, though mercifully rare, have no business being around dogs. Such people seem to exude a subliminal message that can bring out the worst in a canine. Others can knock down spirit just by being present.

Allowing for local work-age restrictions, often the best helpers are high-school students. They often have enough maturity to handle responsibility, but not so much age as to be jaundiced in their views or set in their ways. Especially promising are those youngsters who come looking for work, as many do, instead of waiting for you to come find them. They are the ones who often seem to have a sense of direction, a notion of where they want to go. Moreover, they feel drawn to working with animals generally and dogs specifically. That's why they aren't filling out employment applications at the local fast-food stop or the car wash.

High schoolers are not only in an affordable age bracket; many are willing to learn that there is more to properly taking care of dogs than having a genuine love for them (though that is an essential). Their minds are open and receptive. They have yet to establish bad habits vis-à-vis man's best friend. Many young people I have interviewed are bored silly with school, and are seeking knowledge they see as being potentially useful, something beyond "how to figure the square root of an isosceles triangle (invaluable in daily life)."*

*From *Life 101* by John-Roger and Peter McWilliams (Los Angeles: Bantam Books/Prelude Press, 1991), p. 3.

The good ones are loyal, reliable and not put off by hard work. Also, they can see your operation with fresh eyes and may often come up with solutions for problems that your experience may prevent you from solving. That may seem a paradox, but have you ever tried for a long time to figure out how to do something, and then had an outsider comment, "Well, here's what I would do," and discover that the idea was a good one? I have, and have seen in retrospect that my mind-set born of experience was what prevented me from seeing the obvious.

The question for us is how to spot the winners and how to cull those who are either out of their element or are chasing myths. My manner of selection is far from scientific, but it seems to work well. All interviews are oral—no forms are involved—and take place in and around the kennel, not across a desk in an office.

Gender, race and so forth are of no more concern than is parental social status or school grade-point average. A shy manner is tolerable, withdrawn is not; calmness of spirit is desirable, but a chatterbox is not necessarily a washout. Head-in-the-ozone types need not apply. Formal apparel is not necessary, but spiked hair dyed green indicates more immaturity than I am willing to overlook. Clean, neat, comfortably attired and relaxed of manner is what I want to see.

My first question to the prospect is "Why do you want to work at a kennel?" The answer is of value, of course, but more so is its tone. Allowing for nervousness, which may only mean that the person really wants the job and is feeling pressure from trying to say things "right," I'm looking for calm, collected and decisive in the manner of response. "I dunno" to any question fails the applicant.

My next question is "What would you do if a dog snapped at you while you were petting the animal?" The answer I'm listening for is "Get away from the dog and tell you about the incident." What I don't want to hear is any variation on "Smack the animal in the chops!" An answer like that ends the interview.

My final query, other than obtaining some background material (age, address, next of kin, driver's license, parent's permission—which I get in writing—trouble with the law and if so, for what), is "If you came upon a dog who was vomiting, what would you do?" The answer I am listening for is "Tell you right away." If that is the response I pose a follow-up question: "What if I am not around?" "Call a vet" is the correct answer.

Throughout the interview I am cognizant of where the person's attention is: Is it totally on me or does it tend to drift to the dogs occasionally? Though I am not adamant on the point, I prefer that it is drawn to the animals now and then. Respect for one's elders is admirable, but the individual who never breaks eye contact is worrisome; he or she is usually too tense for my liking. Intensity may be desirable in some fields, but relaxed is more useful in the dog business. Besides, I want to see curiosity and affection operating toward the animals.

Some people have objected to my selection process, opining that it is biased toward flunking those who lack initiative and common sense. It is, I agree. It is intended to be that way. One parent called and asked why I would expect someone to know that which has not been taught (such as what to do about a vomiting dog). I saw no point in trying to explain that the dog business is special, for me, at least, in that the folks who seem to do best at it are akin to the dog in the sense that they already "know"; they just have to be asked in a manner they can understand.

> A dog will readily, and happily, comply with any reasonable request. He usually knows already how to do it. The trainer, however, must formulate the request in a manner that is understood by the dog.*

My experience is that the same principle—especially the one contained in the line "He usually knows already how to do it"—applies not just to dogs but to dog people as well, to the good ones, anyway. They are empathetic and intuitive, not impassive or mechanical. When interviewing kennel help and apprentice trainers, good ones are not only what I seek, they are the only ones I will accept. This is not so much a moral decision as it is one of efficiency: If there is scant potential, why bother?

Competitors

Most boarding kennels are operated by sincere people whose primary concern is their guests' welfare. As with any industry, however, there are always exceptions: A minority of boarding establishments are little more than slipshod germ factories wherein the watchword is the almighty dollar. The only saving grace of such operations is that they make for meager competition.

If there is an ill-managed flea farm in your locale, clients may occasionally say something along the lines of "My! Your kennel is certainly nicer than Fred and Ethel's on the other side of town." Irrespective that the person is probably trying to compliment your

---

*Dietmar Schellenberg, *Top Working Dogs—A Training Manual* (Webster, N.Y.: D.C.B. Publishing, 1985) p. 3.

operation to a greater degree than the comment suggests (saying that you have a nicer place than a pigsty is not really saying much), the proper response is to thank your customer for the kind observation about your kennel but without making any disparaging remarks about Fred and Ethel's facility.

What I am getting at here is the time-honored notion of never knocking the competition. To do so is to cast yourself in a bad light: It sounds like you need to put others down to put yourself ahead; that the only way you can appear better is by slandering others, the bottom-line implication of which is that you are not much to start with.

Many people take competition bashing to be insulting: It is as though you are saying, "I'm telling you what to think about Fred and Ethel's Kennels because you aren't smart enough to figure it out yourself." Further, competition knocking is a form of positive advertising for them because it implies that you are worried about what they have to offer. A client might just get curious and go see what that is.

Besides, you can seldom be sure who you are talking to, and what goes around comes around. A person may be boarding with you because the place where he or she usually leaves pooch is full. Putting down other kennel operators can send a message that you are all a bunch of greedy amateurs.

Always stand on your own merits, emphasizing what you can do, not what the other guy cannot do. If your customers wish to say unflattering things about other kennels, that is their option, but remain noncommittal yourself.

Vet Shopping

Should you not be familiar with a local veterinarian, perhaps being new to the area, meet and get to know one prior to need. An after-hours emergency is no time to discover that the doctor whose name you hurriedly gleaned from the yellow pages has an unreasonable fixation on keeping regular office hours.

In choosing a vet, take your own dog for a cursory examination and observe whether the doctor is at ease with pooch. Of equal importance is whether the animal seems at ease with him or her. Should either seem overly uncomfortable with the other, look elsewhere. While there, check out the general cleanliness of the office and the exam rooms. Also, note the attitude of the clinic staff. Should you detect tension, frayed nerves, short tempers or a decidedly lax, disinterested or distracted manner, be on your way.

Not incidentally, during any visits to a veterinarian's office, leave the dog's obedience training in the car. This is not to say that your pet should not observe good manners while in the office, but a trip to the vet's is not the time to require precision heeling, out-of-sight Stays, Stand for Exams and the rest. Believe it or not, I once observed a person telling his dog, "Stay, Stay, Stay," while the good doctor extracted porcupine quills from the hapless animal's muzzle.

Prudence dictates that two vets are better than one, in the sense that when your primary vet is unavailable you should have a reliable backup. As with your main veterinarian, you and your dog should meet and get to know this second person before a need arises.

After-Hours Medical Care

Once you have located a reliable veterinarian and established a relationship with him or her, you need to have an understanding with the individual: If you ever call after hours it is because you are faced with an emergency and you will expect immediate help, including having the doctor come to you if needed, instead of meeting him or her at the office. Accordingly, you need to have the vet's home number, not that of an answering service. A vet who declines to provide you with that telephone number is cause to look for another doctor. A two-in-the-morning attack of torsion is no time to sweat out having been placed interminably on hold by an answering service whose motto is "We could care less."

Of course, you should never call your vet unless you are faced with a problem that you cannot handle. Also, if the doctor entrusts his or her private number to you, never violate that trust by releasing it to anyone.

When your vet plans to be out of town, you should be made aware of the fact so that in the event of an emergency you don't waste precious minutes fruitlessly trying to make contact.

Sure, all this calls for some concessions on your DVM's part, but remember that it is not a one-sided relationship. As professionals, each of you is in a position to do the other a lot of good. Though it is true that to recommend or suggest a veterinarian to your clientele is to split ethical hairs, there is no harm in telling anyone who your vet is, or that you are well pleased with his or her services.

Fire Drills, Sort Of

What would you do if fire broke out in your kennel? Do you have a plan that you have mentally rehearsed to the point of not having to think about what to do should the real thing happen? Uncertainty born of fear can paralyze decision making during a high-stress event; thus, it is wise to plan certain steps.

For instance, which does one do first: try to get the dogs out or call 911? My plan is to get the animals out if at all possible and *then* call the emergency-service number. A kennel can be rebuilt, a dog cannot. Where should the dogs be put? Into a large, fenced yard well away from the building. What if they begin to fight in the yard? Worry about that after calling the fire department. What if a dog panics and refuses to leave the perceived safety of the kennel? Grab and go. What if a dog should resist by snapping at you? Grab, toss and go. What if a dog appears overcome from smoke inhalation? Get the ones who can walk out first, then rescue smoke victims.

Lest there be misunderstanding, I am hardly suggesting that you conduct fire drills, per se. It would be foolhardy at best to release a group of dogs into a large yard merely for practice; you could easily wind up with a war on your hands. As suggested in the first paragraph, a "*mentally* rehearsed" plan is the objective, so that if faced with a seconds-count calamity, you would react rather than have to decide. Further, I am in no way suggesting that a person risk his or her life to save someone's pet, or that a wastebasket fire that can quickly be doused be cause for emptying a kennel. The steps offered apply to a severe fire that necessitates calling for help but which has yet to spread to the point where one cannot evacuate the building at minimal risk.

Vacation Time

Everyone needs to get out of Dodge once in awhile. But what does a boarding kennel operator do about a vacation, especially a person whose operation is not large enough to justify hiring helpers? As it is a 365-day, all-hours business, you cannot just lock the place up and leave. Or can you?

Many small-business owners find they have to do just that. In that you work with living creatures, you cannot exactly hand the keys to a neighbor and ask that he or she look in on the place from time to time. The alternative to occasionally shutting down is to skip taking vacations, become wedded to (or jailed by) the business and wind up working at a level of tiredness that does no one any good, the boarders included.

Of course, *when* and *for how long* you take some time off can make all the difference as far as your clients are concerned. A month in the south of France during your busiest time of year is not a study in shrewd management. But a week or two during a traditionally slow period will cause very few problems in terms of client relations.

ATTITUDE

Image

Successful businesses seldom happen by accident. They usually outdo the competition by offering something the other guy can't, or won't. In a locale having several kennels, what can you offer that your competitors cannot? You have runs, they have runs. Your facilities are clean, perhaps theirs are as well. You are pleasant with people, they are cordial also. So why is one kennel booked up for weeks at a time while the others are just getting by? The answer is contained in this section's title: Attitude.

Now, I am not just talking here about one's attitude toward owners. That's part of it, sure, but it is not the sum. As long as people are treated with courtesy, respect and appreciation, they will allow a "dog person" certain idiosyncracies. To a degree, they expect someone who makes a living with dogs to be somewhat curious (if not a bit touched). The point is that a kennel operator can be the most personable soul in the county, but if he or she exhibits no genuine caring toward the dogs, if the attitude toward the animals is impersonal, indulgent or plastic, the business will not do well.

Think about it for a moment. Put yourself in an owner's place. You have a dog. Perhaps you have raised her from a puppy. She is not an ornament, she is a member of your family. You are about to embark on a vacation and one of your last stops before leaving town is to entrust your pal's care and well-being to a total stranger. Would you rather hand your leash to a "professional business person" or an obviously "caring dog person"? Will you be offended if the kennel owner greets the animal before shaking your hand? Will you feel affronted if the person's concern seems to center more on how your pet is responding to the new surroundings than in chatting with you? To put it another way, how would you feel if you were greeted by a perpetual and practiced smiler who pumped your hand until you wondered if you were going to get it back, who took your dog's leash without much more than a glance at the animal and who talked about her as though she were not there? This person might pet pooch a time or two, but if you look closely you will see that the action is perfunctory rather than heartfelt. That description does not fit anyone with whom I would leave my dog.

Incarceration or Caring Confinement?

When a dog is boarded, she is restricted to a much smaller area than that to which she is likely accustomed. She finds herself in a totally unfamiliar place, her routine altered, in proximity to strangers (canine and human) and her people not with her. It is a stressful situation for the dog, especially the first time she is boarded. The question, though, is whether the animal is in a run or a cell. The determinant lies in attitude—yours.

When a client boards his or her pet with you, he or she is hiring your space, true, but also being purchased is your time, knowledge, understanding, patience and caring. When a new dog arrives, if she is nervous, spend a few moments with her. When you walk through the kennel building, say each dog's name at least once. When you find a spilled water bucket, do not presume that the animal was being mischievous; for all you know it was spilled by accident. When you board a dog to whom you are not particularly drawn, one who perhaps often growls at you for no apparent reason, remember that the animal— by her very nature—is more likely to be reacting than acting, and that maybe a part of the problem lies with you. Perhaps you are unconsciously sending a message that troubles the dog. No, you do not have to tolerate untoward hostility or bad-actor, destructive tendencies, but it is crucial to remember that no dog is with you for the express purpose of gaining your approval. Any kennel operator looks forward to the arrival of some animals and to the departure of others. That is an inevitable truth that has as much to do with human nature as with canine predispositions and habits. At home that dog is a part of the family, which is why the owner is willing to go to the time, trouble and expense of boarding her in the first place. Your end of the bargain is to always remember that—regardless of how you feel about a certain animal—that dog is very important to someone, as your own pets are to you.

Reflection

Ay, in the catalogue ye go for men;
As hounds and greyhounds, mongrels, spaniels, curs,
Sloughs, water-rugs and demi-wolves, are clept
All by the name of dogs: the valued file
Distinguishes the swift, the slow, the subtle,
The housekeeper, the hunter, every one
According to the gift which bounteous nature
Hath in him closed.

William Shakespeare
Macbeth, act 3, sc. 1, line 92

8

Record Keeping

WHETHER A PERSON views bookkeeping and re-
lated tasks as necessary evils or as tools that can provide valuable data
for decision making, the need for basic record keeping for any business
is a fact of life, as the IRS will gleefully attest. I have examined
computerized kennel-accounting systems that are intricate and complex
in structure and which can produce voluminous statistical data. I have
also seen bare-bones bookkeeping consisting of a cardboard box for
receipts and a legal pad for scratching totals. The best type of system
for you is the one with which you are comfortable, and which produces
accurate data and the fewest headaches.

The following outline is of a middle-of-the-road, hand-system
approach for keeping track of income and expense. It can easily be
modified to suit specific needs.

HAND SYSTEMS

Basics

As a starting point, consider the following guidelines to represent
minimum standards.

1. Establish a checking account specifically for the kennel.
2. Deposit all kennel receipts and pay all kennel expenses
   through this checking account.

3. Record in an *Income Journal* all customer transactions.
4. Obtain and keep receipts for all kennel expenditures.
5. Record kennel expenditures in an *Expense Journal*.
6. Summarize selected data monthly from the *Income Journal* and the *Expense Journal* and record the totals on *Summary Sheets*.
7. Total the *Summary Sheets* annually.

Columnar paper, also known as accountant's pads, can serve for both the *Income Journal* and *Expense Journal*, and for the *Summary Sheets*.

Income

An *Income Journal* might have the following column headings:

|Date|Rec#|Client|Days|Rate|Board|Train|Groom|Other|Total|Tax|Due|Paid|Charge|ROA|

Date   The date each boarder went home.

Rec#   The number of the receipt given to the client.

Client   The client's name.

Days   The number of days the client's dog was with you.

Rate   Your daily fee for boarding the dog.

Board   Days multiplied by the *Rate*.

Train   Training fees.

Groom   Grooming fees.

Other   Miscellaneous fees.

Total   This is the total of the *Board, Train, Groom* and *Other* columns.

Tax   This is the *Total* multiplied by the applicable rate of sales tax. If services such as boarding are not subject to sales tax in your area, omit this column.

Due   This is the amount the client owes you. Again, if services are not subject to sales tax in your area, omit this column; the *Total* column reflects the amount due.

Paid   This is the amount received from the client.

Charge   This is the amount unpaid and charged to the client's account, presuming you offer charge accounts for your customers. If you do not, omit this column.

ROA   Enter payments from charge customers in this *Received on Account* column. If you do not offer charge accounts, omit this column.

If boarding is the only service you offer, the *Board* column reflects your boarding revenue; omit the columns labeled *Train, Groom, Other* and *Total*. If you have other services available, create additional *Income Journal* headings for those categories.

Record the appropriate information whenever a client collects his or her pet. At the end of each month, total the columns labeled *Board, Train, Groom, Other, Total, Tax, Due, Paid, Charge* and *ROA*. Verify that the totals for the *Board, Train, Groom* and *Other* columns equal that for the *Total* column. Similarly, the *Total* and the *Tax* column totals should add up to the *Due* total, as should the totals for the *Paid* and the *Charge* columns. Once these totals are in balance, record them on an *Income Summary Sheet* having the following headings:

At the end of a year, enter the total of each column on the line labeled *YEAR*, and verify the amounts using the same proofs for totaling the *Income Journal* monthly.

Month	Board	Train	Groom	Other	Total	Tax	Due	Paid	Charge	ROA
JAN										
FEB										
MAR										
APR										
MAY										
JUN										
JUL										
AUG										
SEP										
OCT										
NOV										
DEC										
YEAR										

Expense

An *Expense Journal* might have the following column headings:

`|Date|Ck#|Payee/For|Amount|Food|Ads|Equip|Travel|Repair|Utils|Ins|Tax|Other|`

Date	The date of the transaction.
Ck#	The check's number.
Payee/For	Who you wrote the check to, or what the check was in payment of, or both.
Amount	The amount of the check.

The remaining headings itemize the categories to which the expenses are charged.

Food	Cost of dog food.
Ads	Advertising.
Equip	Purchases of kennel equipment.
Travel	The cost of getting from one place to another to conduct kennel business.
Repair	The costs of performing repairs and maintenance to the kennel.
Utils	Utility costs, such as electricity and water.
Ins	Insurance expenses.
Tax	Expense of taxes and licenses applicable to the kennel.
Other	Miscellaneous expenses that cannot properly be classified under one of the other headings.

Of course, if other expense categories are applicable to your operation, add additional headings for those expenses.

As with the *Income Journal*, total the amount columns of the *Expense Journal* monthly. The totals of the columns for *Food, Ads, Equip, Travel, Repair, Utils, Ins, Tax* and *Other*—as well as the totals for any other classifications you may have added—should equal the total of the *Amount* column. Once they are in balance, post these totals to an *Expense Summary Sheet*, set up as follows:

Month	Amount	Food	Ads	Equip	Travel	Repair	Utils	Ins	Tax	Other
JAN										
FEB										
MAR										
APR										
MAY										
JUN										
JUL										
AUG										
SEP										
OCT										
NOV										
DEC										
YEAR										

At year end, enter the total for each column on the line labeled *YEAR*, and verify the amounts using the same mathematical proofs for totaling the *Expense Journal* monthly.

Net

Create one final *Summary Sheet*, as follows.

Month	Total Income	Total Expense	Net Gain/<Loss>
JAN			
FEB			
MAR			
APR			
MAY			
JUN			
JUL			
AUG			
SEP			
OCT			
NOV			
DEC			
YEAR			

In the column labeled *Total Income*, enter the amounts from the *Total* column of your *Income Summary Sheet*. In the column labeled *Total Expense*, enter the amounts from the *Amount* column of your *Expense Summary Sheet*. Subtract the amount of *Total Expense* from the *Total Income* for each month, entering the results in the *Net Gain/ <Loss>* column. The total of the *Net Gain/<Loss>* column should equal the year's *Total Income* minus the year's *Total Expense*.

It's Up to You

Not incidentally, the use of *Summary Sheets* can be skipped, if you wish. One can merely total the *Income Journal* annually to determine the year's sales. However, should the columns not balance, a year's worth of bookkeeping has to be audited to locate the errors. Posting monthly totals to a *Summary Sheet* calls for an extra step but can greatly simplify year-end work.

Another form of refinement is to delete the columns labeled *Board, Train, Groom* and *Other* from the *Income Journal* and from the *Income Summary Sheet*. Merely enter all sales into the *Total* column. Categorizing of sales is internal information that may be of no interest to the IRS.* However, expenses must be itemized by category, so it would be unwise to consider also eliminating the expense breakdowns (*Food, Ads, Equip, Travel, Repair, Utils, Ins, Tax* and *Other*) from the *Expense Journal* and from the *Expense Summary Sheet*.

One Final Record

If you allow clients to charge their accounts, maintain a ledger containing an account sheet for each individual. A sample account sheet might appear as follows:

Name:		Address:			
City:	State:	Zip:	Phone:		
Date	Detail		Charge	Credit	Balance

Date	The date of each charge and each payment.
Detail	The dog's name and the from–to dates of service.
Charge	The amount charged to the account for this transaction from the *Charge* column in the *Income Journal*.
Credit	Payments as recorded in the *ROA* column of the *Income Journal*.
Balance	This is the total of the previous balance (if any) plus *Charges* minus *Credits*.

The total of all account balances should equal the previous total of such balances plus current *Income Journal* charges minus current *Income Journal* ROAs.

*There are some exceptions to this; check with a tax professional.

Overview

Diagrammed, the foregoing system appears as follows:

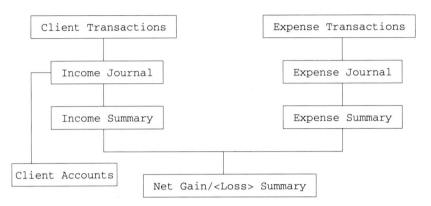

Internal Data

Internal records and reports reflect information that you may not be required by law to keep, but which can be useful for the effective management of your business. Though the types of reports are limited only by need and imagination, consider the following statistical analysis.

Date	#Runs	Month	Year	Avail	%Occup	Dogs	Month	Year	PerRun	NoVac

Date	Refers to the current day's date.
#Runs	The number of runs occupied on that date.
Month	The number of runs occupied so far for the current month.
Year	The number of runs occupied so far for the current year.
Avail	The number of runs available for occupancy so far for the current year.
%Occup	The *Year* total expressed as a percentage of the *Avail* total.
Dogs	The number of dogs boarded on that date.
Month	The number of dogs boarded so far for the current month.

148

Year	The number of dogs boarded so far for the current year.
PerRun	The number of dogs boarded so far for the current year divided by the number of runs occupied for the same period, the idea being to determine the average number of dogs occupying each rented run.
NoVac	The number of customers you have had to turn away because all your runs were booked when they contacted you to make a reservation.

Create a summary sheet for recording the preceding data on a monthly/annual basis; simply replace the *Date* column with one reading *Month*. The usefulness of a report like this is to reflect how your boarding operation is doing at any given time, to provide comparisons between months and years and to determine seasonal trends. No-vacancy figures can indicate whether your operation should be expanded.

Utilities Expenses

There is but one foolproof way of accurately accounting for a kennel's utilities expenses: installing separate meters. As that can be quite expensive, however, an alternative method is to apportion utilities on a percentage basis. For example, if your home has X square feet and the kennel building has Y square feet, the result of Y divided by X-plus-Y will yield the kennel's percentage of square feet to the total square feet. This percentage can then be applied to your utility bills to determine how much of the expense should be allocated to the kennel.

I offer one caution when using the percentage method, however: Visit with a tax professional before instituting the procedure. Tax law changes like the seasons, and by the time you read this book it may be that the percentage method cannot legally be used. Further, it may be that the percentage method is not realistic in terms of your particular facility. If your kennel has one one-hundred-watt light bulb that is only used for a couple of hours nightly, many tax agencies might object to your claim that—based on the percentage of square feet—your kennel is using, say, 25 percent of your monthly electric bill. As I said, check with a tax pro before instituting any method of determining utilities costs.

A related utility expense is that of long-distance calls. Keep a log showing the date of each call, to whom it was made and the purpose of each call. When your telephone bill arrives, match expense with logged calls.

Date	To	For	Start	End	Miles

Mileage Record Keeping

Maintain a sheet for recording the following kennel mileage-related information, using the following headings:

Date For recording the date of the trip.
To Where you went.
For The purpose of the trip.
Start The beginning mileage on the vehicle's odometer.
End The ending mileage on the vehicle's odometer.
Miles The number of miles driven during the trip (*End* minus *Start*).

Summary

The purpose of the foregoing system is to provide a simple set of tools for determining how your business is succeeding, and to establish a paper trail you can follow should substantiation of your records ever be necessary.

COMPUTERIZED SYSTEMS

They Byte, But They Don't Bite

While it is true that a person can successfully operate a kennel without knowing a personal computer from a box of Rice Krispies, it is equally true that a computer can simplify many of the mundane record-keeping tasks required by various governmental agencies. Computers are not creations of demons and sorcerers; they are machines, nothing more. As one wit recently observed, "If Joel can successfully run a computer, anyone can." To adapt such a machine to the kennel business, one need not be a computer guru. All that is needed is a working knowledge of three types of software (programs), which I have ranked in order of overall usefulness to a boarding kennel operation: spreadsheets, data bases and word processors.

Spreadsheet Software

Spreadsheet software is used to manipulate numbers and create graphs. Two better-known programs are *Lotus 1-2-3* and *Quattro Pro*.

150

However, both are more powerful than most boarding kennel operations would ever need, are quite expensive and are less than user-friendly. The market offers many less sophisticated spreadsheet programs that have more than adequate power and capabilities, and which sport lower price tags. I personally rely on *V-P Planner 3D*, a program that has been discontinued but can still be located through some software outlets.

The on-screen appearance of a spreadsheet is similar to its paper counterpart—columns and rows, as below:

Lest appearances deceive, computer spreadsheets are considerably larger than the sample section shown above. Many are 256 columns wide by 8,192 rows long. True, one could settle for recording data on a columnar pad, but the advantages of computer spreadsheet usage are speed (i.e., time saved), mathematical accuracy and storage capacity. My routine bookkeeping chores take less than two minutes a day and about fifteen minutes at month's end. At any given time, two keystrokes provide me with the following information:

Revenue today
Revenue to date for the month
Revenue to date for the year
Last year's month- and year-to-date revenue, for comparisons
The five-year average month and average year-to-date revenue
Projected monthly and annual revenue

The program also provides similar data concerning the number of runs rented for the day, month and year, and percentage of occupancy for the same periods. Daily it updates my current-year federal income-tax return.

Data-Base Software

Another type of recommended program is a data base. It is similar to spreadsheet software—an experienced user can make either do the work of the other—and it beats the daylights out of index-card usage. Of the several programs that I have tried, my preference in terms of power, adaptability and ease of use is *Alpha4*. Once the program is installed on a computer and data has been recorded, you can use it to list clients by name, by dog's name, by dates of arrival (or departure), by breeds of dog or by any other combination of criteria you specify. I have my software configured such that by typing the client's name, the following information appears on screen in less than three seconds:

Client's name
Spouse's name
Address
City
State
Zip code
Telephone
Dog's name
Breed
Dog's gender
Any notations about specific needs or problems with this client or dog
A complete history of this client's arrival and departure dates and times, and amounts charged
How many times the dog has been boarded with me
The total amount spent to date by the client
The average amount spent per visit

When dealing with hundreds of clients, it can be difficult to recall each and every person and dog. That's when something as impersonal as a computer can personalize your relationship with clients. For instance, the phone rings, and the caller says, ''Hi, this is John Jones calling.'' While you respond with, ''Well, hello, Mr. Jones. How have you been?'' you type his name into the computer. By the time he has replied, ''Oh, real good, thank you,'' you have the aforementioned data on screen and can ask, ''How's my friend Old Buster, your Airedale?'' That can make a very positive impression, especially when you have not seen the dog for several months.

In addition to providing you with quick information, a data-base program can be used to create mailing labels, form letters and billing statements. Further, the software can be instructed to print mailing labels, for instance, only for clients who meet certain criteria, such as those who have done business with you during the past year, or owners of Fox Terriers, or clients who live in a certain area, or virtually any other criteria you want.

Word-Processing Software

A third type of program that can prove useful is word-processing software. Many word-processing programs can directly use information from spreadsheet and data-base files, which eliminates the need for duplicate entries and allows the user to produce more professional-looking letters and other documents than can be generated from data-base programs. *WordPerfect, Ami Pro* and *MicroSoft Word* are some of the better-known word-processor packages. *WordPerfect* is my choice, to the extent that I have used it in writing each of my books. All of the forms presented in this book, as well as all forms in use at my kennels, were created using *WordPerfect* software.

DOS

DOS (rhymes with "toss") is an abbreviation for Disk Operated System. It is software that allows a computer to operate. It is not necessary to be a DOS expert to effectively and efficiently run a computer, but life with computers is a lot easier with knowledge of a few basic commands, such as Format, Copy and Diskcopy. My preferred operating software is MS-DOS, the "MS" standing for Micro-Soft.

Clip Art

Clip art is artwork that can be used by other programs. The market offers literally thousands of clip-art images. I incorporated the following eye-catcher into this *WordPerfect* document in less time than it took to type this sentence.

*Graphic used with permission of *WordPerfect* Corporation, Orem, Utah.

Other Software

PrintMaster is one of the better graphics programs available. Graphics software can be used to create banners, posters, calendars, letterheads and the like.

Also potentially useful is desktop-publishing software, newsletters and brochures being but two possible applications. *WordPerfect* can be used for limited DTP work, but *Publish It!* from Timeworks Software is more versatile.

Canis, an excellent program for record keeping, resource information and all-around enjoyment, is available from Centron Software Technologies (Deerfield Beach, Fla.).

Breeders should also be aware that programs for tracking breeding records and genetic data are available, as is software for reproducing pedigrees.

Protect Yourself

If you do use a computer, back up your data files onto floppy disks (or magnetic tape) often, preferably daily. The process, which can be automated, takes only a few minutes and can save hours should your primary storage device (usually a hard disk) fail. Also, print and store your data at least monthly; weekly is even better.

Though I always keep a set of back-up disks at my residence, storing additional back-up files at a location other than one's home or business is a sound plan. Once a week I put several floppy disks in my safe-deposit box at the bank. At the same time I take home the disks that I placed in the box a week earlier, erasing them to record next week's back-up files. My thought is that I am never risking more than a week's data to the possibility of loss through fire.

Overlap

If you presently maintain books by hand but plan to convert to computerized record keeping, plan on running parallel (both) systems for several weeks or months. Continue to maintain your present hand system until such time as you feel totally confident and at ease in operating your computer and its software.

Shopping List

What is a "computer system"? A basic system consists of the following hardware:

Computer	Known in the trade as "the box," this is the unit that contains the electronic gadgetry that allows all other equipment (monitor, keyboard, printer and so forth) to work together.
Monitor	This is the video screen.
Keyboard	Akin in appearance to the result of breeding a typewriter keyboard with a ten-key adding-machine keyboard, this unit is used by an operator to send information and commands to the computer.
Printer	This device prints information from the computer onto paper.
RAM	An abbreviation for Random Access Memory, these are electronic chips on which information is stored temporarily.
Hard Disk	Also known as a hard drive, this is an internal disk on which data is stored until and if a user wants to remove the data.
Graphics Card	Also housed within the computer, this is an electronic device that permits the computer to transmit information to the monitor.
Floppy-Disk Drive	This is a slot in the computer casing into which floppy disks can be inserted; like a hard disk, floppy disks store data, though in considerably lesser quantities than a hard disk. A floppy disk can store thousands of words; a hard disk can store millions.
Surge Suppressor	Often termed a "surge strip," this is a unit which all other devices that need electricity are plugged into. Its purpose is to protect delicate equipment against the potentially damaging effects of power fluctuations. Don't ever operate your computer unless it and your peripheral equipment are plugged into such a device.

Buying a Computer System

So not to leave you hanging, here are a few tips about purchasing a computer system. First, recognize the truism that computer technology changes faster than politicians change their tunes. Many of the thoughts

I offer may be obsolete by the time this book goes to press. Accordingly, if you have a trusted friend who is knowledgeable about computers, share this section of *Kennels and Kenneling* with him or her and ask for the individual's help and advice.

Unless you are an experienced user, the first suggestion I offer a prospective computer owner is to buy locally. Yes, money can be saved through mail-order houses, and though some are very ethical and supportive, others are less so. I have several years of experience with computer hardware and software, and though I could shop through the mail, I want a local dealer standing behind my equipment.

That leads to suggestion number two, which is an extension of number one: Deal with a reputable, established business that is well equipped and is staffed by knowledgeable, experienced technicians. The type of computer store I have in mind not only warrants its merchandise for an acceptable period, it will provide loaner equipment at no charge if a system it sold has to be in the shop longer than overnight for repair. Should a computer salesperson assure you that "If your system fails we'll have it back from the factory in no time," get gone. What the individual is saying is that you may just as well deal with a mail-order house. A dealer whose best solution for faulty equipment is making you wait while the unit is sent away for repairs is offering you mail-order service at local-dealer prices. You want to trade with someone who can handle his or her own minor repairs, and who will replace defective equipment needing major work.

In finding a salesperson, look for one who speaks your language and who doesn't push you. If someone constantly tries to overwhelm you with technical terms and buzz words, or who tries to pressure you into a decision you are not ready to make, shop elsewhere. Also, be wary of those who try to sell you more hardware or software (machines or programs) than you need. This is where the advice of a trusted friend mentioned earlier can be invaluable. Such salespeople often speak of a certain peripheral gadget as being "the wave of the future." A person having that kind of vision would be running a computer company, not peddling hardware. Am I suggesting that there are some hucksters in the computer-sales industry? If there were not, it would be the only form of business devoid of such occasional parasites.

The system you purchase should be fully assembled and tested at the store; the testing period (known as "burn-in time") should last at least seventy-two hours. All software should be installed for you and the purchase price should include delivery, setup and at least two hours of training. The store should offer nominally priced classes about the software you are purchasing, and should be more than willing to provide you with a list of customers who have bought similar systems from them.

The foregoing are general suggestions; here are a few specifics. Shop for a computer that is 100 percent (that's a key phrase: "100 percent") IBM-compatible. For our purposes, an IBM-compatible computer (often known as an "IBM clone") is so designated because it will handle any IBM-based software. It does not carry the IBM name, but neither does it display a whimsical price tag. My preference in this type of machine are the computers distributed by the Hewitt-Rand Corporation.

Hard-disk size is important in two ways. Too small a hard drive will ultimately have to be replaced; too large a unit represents wasted investment dollars. Most boarding kennel operators should find the best value in drives ranging in size from sixty to one hundred megabytes. My preference for reliability, warranty period and cost are the hard drives made by the Quantum Corporation.

Unless you have money to burn, the best type of printing device is a *dot-matrix* style of printer. Laser-technology printers produce beautiful copy quickly and quietly, but they are also quite expensive. Panasonic offers excellent dot-matrix quality; their KX-P1124i model should adapt well to most boarding kennel offices. If you want a wide-carriage printer, look at Panasonic's model KX-P1624. Should you decide that you must have a laser printer, my favorites are the Hewlett-Packard LaserJet models III and IV.

An item known as a math co-processor chip is not necessary for the system I have described. Though it is indisputable that a math-co dramatically hastens arithmetic calculations, often by as much as several hundred percent, remember that such speed increases sound very impressive but that the real-world time difference is measurable in seconds or even in microseconds.

Last, I do not prefer the Windows style of computing. Stay with DOS-based (preferably MS-DOS) software. To my mind, Windows is an unnecessary and expensive complication for a small business like a boarding kennel.

They Are Known as "Home Computers"

If there is the slightest chance that your computer could be subject to water damage in your kennel, keep the device and all related equipment in your home. Water and electronics don't mix.

Chapter Omissions

This chapter has not directly addressed such specialized topics as tax law, depreciation schedules and mileage allowances. Regulations pertaining to these and similar issues are changed too frequently to be included in a general book on kennel operation. My best recommendation for advice about such matters is to do what I do when confused about an issue concerning tax matters: Seek the help of a tax professional.

Reflection

Order and simplification are the first steps toward the mastery of a subject—the actual enemy is the unknown.

Thomas Mann
The Magic Mountain

9

Problems and Solutions

THIS CHAPTER could have been incorporated into chapter 7, "Policies, Practices and Direction." That chapter's topics, however, are generally broader in nature than are the following "What if?" scenarios. Not everything occurs in a nice, neat and orderly fashion in the boarding kennel business (nor in any other that I know of), and it is therefore difficult if not impossible to formulate all-encompassing, infallible policies; not every contingency can be foreseen. This chapter of *Kennels and Kenneling* attempts to fill that gap by covering a number of the oddball matters that have a way of popping up from time to time. It also covers things that go bump in the night, or the day, or at any time in between.

Problem: A caller asks if it is alright to bring a dog bed or blanket for pooch.

Solution: Tell the individual, "Of course, it is," and be glad you are dealing with a thoughtful owner. When new clients call, in fact, if they don't raise the subject of bringing a little bit of home with them for their pet, you should. Ask if the animal has a favorite blanket or rug that he sleeps on, and if he does, suggest that the owner bring it along. If the dog has no such article, provide one for him. It is a small touch, but one that makes for a more comfortable, calmer boarder.

Problem: A dog, for whatever reason, attempts to chew or rip his blanket (or similar article).

Solution: Regardless of whether the item was provided by you or brought by the owner, remove it from his run. Ingestion of cloth can be fatal.

Problem: The animal fouls the blanket or dog bed that the owner brought from home.

Solution: Clean it. Sure, the animal should not have soiled his sleeping area, but that is beside the point. Don't ever send a dog or his bed home dirty.

Problem: A boarder who is soon due to go home has taken on what is commonly referred to as a "kennel smell."

Solution: Bathe and dry the animal shortly before the owner is scheduled to return. Though in most cases one could argue that the condition is the dog's "fault"—he may not have the cleanest habits imaginable—that is not the problem. The problem is that the dog smells, and an owner detecting the odor will not conclude that it is of his pet's doing; he will conclude that you run a smelly kennel.

By the way, unless the service was requested when the dog arrived, do not try to charge the owner for bathing the animal. You may or may not be able to collect, but the odds are high that you will alienate the client over the issue; the person may feel that he is being nicked because you don't run a clean kennel. A way to handle this element—collecting a fee for bathing the animal—is to make yourself a note to ask the owner the next time he arrives if he would like his dog bathed prior to going home. That way you have a chance of being paid for the minor grooming service should it be needed in the future.

Problem: Your feeding policy is twice a day and removing the food bowls after a set interval (say, ten minutes), regardless of whether each dog has eaten his meal. But a client tells you that he puts down his dog's only in the morning, and that the animal is a nibbler, eating a little bit every so often throughout the day. What should you do?

Solution: Respect the client's wishes. Imposing your meal policy on a few-days' boarder almost guarantees that the dog will not eat during his stay. The exception to this rule would be the dog whose owner provides the food, and the food is a malodorous concoction that attracts an impressive number of flies.

Problem: A boarder who has been eating well suddenly goes off his feed for several meals. Is this cause for concern?

Solution: One of the first signs of canine illness is the tendency to quit eating. Though it is not a definitive symptom, call the client's vet—or your own if the owner's DVM is not available—and let the doctor advise you as to the best steps to take.

Problem: A boarder consistently spills his food dish, sending kibble scattering in all directions. He eats well enough, but only after upsetting his food bowl.

Solution: Don't worry about it. The animal is with you for boarding, not training. It is likely that he does the same thing at home, and so long as he is getting proper nourishment, his flip-the-dish habit is more his problem than yours.

Problem: A caller advises you that her dog is on medication for allergies, that the animal requires umpteen pills and liquids throughout the day and that "He's not real good about taking his medicine sometimes, heh, heh, heh."

Solution: Ask the owner what she means about the dog being "not real good." If you are told that the animal "Might nip at you once in awhile," mentally translate that into "The dog will try to bite me every time," and turn down the business. If the owner says that the creature is "just stubborn, turns his head away" and so on, then you have to decide whether you want to put up with the hassle of dealing with a recalcitrant animal several times a day. Also, be aware that a dog who is stubborn with his owner may be aggressive toward you, a stranger.

If you decide to board the dog, ask the owner to have her veterinarian call you. You want to be sure that the allergy is not some other problem, like a contagious disease. Then call your own vet and verify the facts as they have been explained to you by the owner's DVM. If your veterinarian communicates negative feelings about the dog's condition, realize that your first concern is for the boarders already in your kennel, and tactfully turn down the business.

Problem: An owner arrives to collect pooch and advises, "I forgot my checkbook at home. Can I mail you a check?"

Solution: If the individual is an established client, sure. This kind of thing can happen to anyone, as can finding oneself out of checks, having forgotten to insert a new booklet after writing the last check in a series.

If the person is a new customer but the account is quite small, I would take a chance on the person's honesty. Refusing to release a dog over a small amount may get you the cash but lose you the client.

If the owner is a first-time client who has a sizable account, go with what your gut tells you. Ofttimes that's what running a business is all about. Yes, the person may be trying to get to you, or he or she may prove to be a valued customer. A large tab seems risky when you are being asked to take an IOU, but at the same time it may be that the account is large because the individual is willing to spend considerable sums with you. Keep in mind always, though, that if things do not seem on the up and up to you, if you have a bad feeling about the situation, you are well within your rights to keep the client's pet until you have been paid.

Problem: A client's check bounces.

Solution: If the check was returned with the notation "NSF" ("Non-Sufficient Funds"), contact the client and discuss the situation. Perhaps there was a mix-up while the individual was on vacation. If the check was returned marked "Account Closed," insist that the client bring you the cash forthwith, or offer to drive to the client's home to make the collection. This person may be about to move from the area, which would likely leave you holding the bag.

As a corollary, become familiar with credit practices and legal recourses in your area. Find out what your rights are in the cases of bad checks or nonpayment.

Problem: An owner arrives to get his pet and advises you that he is unable to pay.

Solution: Keep the dog until you get the cash. Don't take a check from this person. Of course, if the client has a good history with you, you may wish to show more trust than I am recommending. My experience, though, is that reliable people who are temporarily short of funds tend to make arrangements for payment when they call to make a reservation or when they arrive with their pet, not when they come to take the animal home.

Problem: A client who was scheduled to be back two days hence arrives today in the late afternoon to collect her pet and tells you that she came by that morning to pick up pooch but that you were not there. It is true that you were in town that morning to get dog food, but given that your check-out hour is one o'clock, do you charge the customer for today?

Solution: No. Even if the individual were to arrive that evening to get her pet, she should not be charged for today. You should be glad that the person is not upset that you were not at the kennel when she came by earlier. Apologize that your absence caused the client to have to make an additional trip, and thank her for her business.

Problem: After a client has departed for home with his pet, you discover an error in the amount you charged.

Solution: If you undercharged the client by a small amount, such as one day's boarding, forget it; don't pester the customer. Mutter something to yourself on the order of "You'd think by now I'd know two and two don't equal three," and forget it. It's a small thing. If the amount in question is significant, contact the individual and explain the problem. Most people will understand. If you overcharged the client by any amount, small or large, contact him right away and offer to send a check or, if he would prefer, to credit his account against the next visit.

Problem: After a client takes his or her pet home, you discover that you forgot to return an item of equipment (food dish, blanket, toy, etc.).

Solution: Call the customer, apologize and offer to bring the forgotten item to the client's home.

Problem: A client, while getting ready to take her pet home, tells you to keep the small amount of remaining food she furnished for the visit, that she does not want to be bothered taking it home, to give it to the other dogs, that "They'll like it!" It is an acceptable brand of food, but one that you would not feed to your own dogs (i.e., or to other boarders).

Solution: This one is not really so much of a problem as it is an opportunity. True, you could just thank the customer and throw out the food after she departs, but give it to your local animal shelter instead. "They'll like it!"

Problem: A client told you three weeks ago that he would be back sometime this afternoon to pick up his pooch. It is 4:30 P.M., and the store that called to say that your eagerly awaited whatsis has finally arrived closes at 5:00 P.M. It is a Saturday and the store will be closed until Monday. What do you do?

Solution: Stay put. Your clients and their pets come first. Settle for looking forward to getting your whatsis on Monday.

Let's make it trickier: Suppose the client is one who tends to arrive when he gets there; he seldom sticks to his planned schedule. Now what's the answer?

It's still "Stay put," for the reasons given.

Problem: You have locked up the kennel, the morning's labors are behind you and you are about ready to leave for a mini-break in the form of a luncheon engagement in town with a friend. Just as you are walking out the door a client calls, asking if he or she can bring Poopsie out within the hour for a few days of boarding.

Solution: First, you must accept the reservation (presuming you have an unoccupied run). If it is not convenient for the person to bring the dog to you later in the day, you might ask about picking up the animal on your way back to the kennel. If that is not suitable for your client, you have two options: Call your friend and see if your lunch date can be moved ahead an hour, or postpone the engagement until another time. Sure, it would have been nice for the client to have given you more notice, but like a hotel, when a caller wants to do business you have to be ready to accept it.

Problem: You have a full kennel, and a client of long standing calls to tell you that he or she forgot to make a reservation (or, "I thought my better half had made a reservation"). "Can you help me out?"

Solution: You cannot afford not to. Experience teaches that there is almost always room for one more. Somehow, someway, find room for that dog.

A similar situation that can occur involves the owner who arrives claiming that he or she made a reservation weeks ago but you have no record of it. The solution is the same: Find a way to board the dog. You could have forgotten to properly record the reservation.

Problem: A client calling at three o'clock in the morning has a family emergency, and "Can you take Old Buster?"

Solution: Find a way to board that dog. Even if you have a full kennel, tell the caller that you will turn on a light and will be waiting. People do not call in such a circumstance unless their backs are up against a wall, and you cannot afford to turn them down at those times.

Problem: What do you do if a client does not return? It is a fluke, to be sure, but it can happen. Though accidents and fatal illness would seem to be the most likely causes, I have never known either to occur. What I have experienced is owners who left pooch with me, departed and were never heard from again. Obviously they had planned not to come back. Either they could not find a home for their pet, or could not be bothered to look for one, and rather than take the animal to the shelter, they dropped him off with good old me. This has happened to me three times over the years; it may happen to you. The question in such a circumstance is, of course, "Now what?"

Solution: First, wait at least a week, preferably two, before taking any action. Be sure that the owners are not likely to return; that they were not merely delayed and did not think to call you. Second, recognize that the occurrence is not the dog's fault. He just lost his family (though it may not have been much of a loss), and he does not need any further rejection. Be careful not to communicate negative vibrations to him. Third, send the owners a registered letter, return receipt requested, at their last known address. Inform them that if they do not claim their pet within a certain number of days,* the animal will be put to sleep and you will sue them for the cost of boarding and for the cost of euthanasia. Then, after the stipulated time has past, get to work at finding the animal a good home. No, we are not going to put that dog down—that is simply not an option. The threat is put in the letter only to shake up the clowns who abandoned their pet, assuming they indeed receive your message. Once you locate a home for the dog you may be able to recover some of the boarding fees from the new owners. If you cannot, though, let the dog go with the realization that his new people may someday board him with you. Yes, you will then lose a few dollars, but bad debts are part of running any business. Accept the loss, realize that you did good by finding pooch a home and get on with your day.

Problem: You need to run next door to a neighbor's home for just long enough to drop off an item they loaned you. Since you will only be gone for a few minutes, do you need to go through the rigmarole of padlocking all runs and locking the kennel building and the perimeter-fence gates?

Solution: Yes. There are some chances one never takes; this is one of them. Sure, the neighbor lives close by and you will make your trip a quick one, but consider: Dog thieves do exist, they see places like yours as a potential gold mine and they can be very quick themselves.

---

*Check with a local attorney on this one. Regulations vary from state to state on how long you have to wait before assuming ownership of an abandoned dog.

Problem: You have to leave the kennel for a few minutes. Do you put all the dogs inside, or do you leave their run access doors open so they can enjoy the bright, sunny day if they wish?

Solution: Put the dogs inside. Protection of the animals comes before concerns for exercise or sunbathing. Granted, the odds are very high that everything would be fine, but for all you know some sicko with a high-powered rifle is just waiting for you to leave.

Problem: You have to be away from the kennel for a few hours to pick up supplies. Is there any reason to padlock the gates of the unoccupied runs as well as those of the occupied ones?

Solution: Yes. If someone with devious intent were to crawl over your perimeter fence during your absence, padlocked runs make it far more difficult to get at a run access door to break into the building. Also, a thief might correctly interpret an unlocked run as being empty. Make it appear that all runs are occupied, and let an intruder sweat out which run access door might have a bad-tempered, large, unfriendly dog waiting behind it.

Problem: You have to be away from the kennel for a time and know that clients may be arriving during your absence. Do you leave a note on your gate stating when you expect to return?

Solution: Though it may seem courteous to do so, security concerns come first, and it is wiser not to advertise: 1) that you are not there, and 2) how long someone with evil intent has to cause you harm.

Problem: A prospective client visiting your kennel comments, "My! What a beautiful Lhasa Apso you have in that run there. Can I step into the run and pet the adorable little dog?"

Solution: Though you do not have to share the sentiment's qualifier with the visitor, the answer to some questions is not just "No," but "Hell, no!" This is one such question. No one—and I mean no one—except you, your kennel helpers or a veterinarian should ever be allowed contact with any boarder. Others may look but they may not touch.

Now, a question that can arise is, "What if the person who wants to pet the dog is a longtime client, not a stranger?" The answer is still the same: No. Sure, everything is probably on the up and up, but consider: What if the dog were to bite the person? Or, what if the individual fell and suffered an injury while in the run? In either case you could find yourself on the receiving end of a lawsuit.

Problem: A stranger appears at your gate. He or she tells you that you have a beautiful kennel and asks to look around. You notice that the person's vehicle is carrying out-of-state (or out-of-county) license plates. Well?

Solution: Deflect the request by telling the individual that you just don't have time at the moment, but "Perhaps you could come back later." Ask a few questions along the theme of "Do you live around here?" If the answer is no, then ferret out why the person wants to visit your kennel. There are hundreds of legitimate reasons why someone from another area might want to look over your kennel. Perhaps the individual is thinking of building one herself, was sincere in her opening compliment and is looking for some pointers. But those are pretty precious dogs in your care, and it is safer in terms of their protection to err on the side of caution in all dealings with unknowns.

A question that may occur to you about now is, "Is he making these scenarios up, or do they reflect experience?" Answer: My imagination is good, but it is not that good. Dog thieves are not only a reality, in many cases they are well organized and are quite skillful at what they do. I am not suggesting that every stranger be treated as a possible crook. I am saying that every stranger is someone whom you do not know the first thing about, by definition, and that until you do know something about the individual, tread very softly. Though neither is desirable, it is better to be a little standoffish than to risk the security of someone's pet.

Problem: A dog injures himself while in your care, perhaps nicking a leg on chain-link while trying to escape (don't think it can't happen). Who pays the vet bill?

Solution: You do. Yes, it was the dog's "fault," but that is a truth of a kind. The animal was *in your care*. Presenting an owner with a bill for a few stitches and some antibiotics for an injury received while at your facility almost guarantees that you will not see that person—or his or her friends—again, though you may become acquainted with the individual's attorney.

Problem: A dog develops kennel cough a few days after being taken home. Who pays for his treatment?

Solution: You do, or at least you make the offer. Point out that no other boarders have developed the condition, but don't ever leave an owner with a memory of his or her dog getting sick at your kennel, and "They didn't do anything about it."

Problem: A dog becomes ill while in your care and you have less than total confidence in the client's veterinarian. Who do you contact for treatment? The client's vet, or yours?

Solution: Only if you cannot locate the DVM the client has specified, do you enlist the aid of your veterinarian. To take a dog to your vet without trying to reach the client's preferred veterinarian is not only out of line ethically, it exposes you to legal repercussions should the animal become more sick or die. Besides, the client's vet already knows the dog and the animal's history. To arbitrarily decide that your vet is more qualified to treat a dog that he or she has never seen is to presume knowledge that most boarding kennel operators do not have.

Problem: A dog seriously damages a portion of chain-link paneling at your kennels. Who pays the repair bill?

Solution: Certainly not the owner. Your facilities are supposed to be such that a dog cannot damage them—that is what an owner would likely tell you were you to present a bill for any repairs. We both know that there are dogs who can damage chain-link (or nearly any other material), but that is not the owner's problem: It is ours. You might want to make a mental note not to take the dog for boarding in the future, however.

Problem: A dog escapes from your facility.

Solution: Find him. Contact neighbors, place ads, mobilize friends and law-enforcement people, and the National Guard if you can arrange it, but find that dog! No other answer is acceptable.

As a corollary, if you did not see the animal run off but merely came upon the empty run, it is possible that the dog was stolen and you should advise law-enforcement personnel accordingly, to give them a fuller picture of the situation's possibilities.

Problem: A dog who is scheduled to be with you for several days or weeks refuses to eat.

Solution: For a dog in strange surroundings to ignore an initial meal—or even as many as four (at a rate of two feeding times daily)—is neither unusual nor cause for concern. With an animal who shuns food beyond that point, however, special steps should be taken.

Offering a piece of kibble from your cupped (for safety) hand to a depressed animal will often get the ball rolling, as will putting a single bite on the floor of the indoor run for a nervous one. Contact operates in the first situation, curiosity in the second one. Should either technique have the desired result, repeat it several times, then place the food bowl in front of pooch's nose, depart and let nature take its course.

Briefly rubbing a few bits of kibble along the dog's back before presenting them to him can be an effective fast-breaker. The food absorbs the animal's scent, thereby marking it as "safe." Another useful technique is pouring over kibble a solution of a tablespoon of hamburger stirred to obscurity while heated in a cup of water (but allow the liquid to cool before giving the food to the dog). Meat juice dripped over kibble can be equally effective. Should a dog refuse nourishment for three days, however, contact the client's veterinarian, at least as a precautionary move.

Problem: You discover that a boarder is a stool eater.

Solution: Keep the animal's run free of stools, thereby eliminating the problem. Sure, you clean the runs several times daily as it is, but keep an eye on this particular dog so you can tell when his run should be cleaned again.

Problem: You board a dog who consistently eliminates in his indoor run, where he sleeps.

Solution: Keep the animal outside as much as possible, and be grateful that he is not your pet.

Problem: A dog is a perpetual fence fighter, initiating a war with his neighbors at the drop of a hat.

Solution: Move the fighter to another run, preferably to one that is adjacent to an empty run. If that is not possible, briefly turn a (cold) water hose on the animal the instant he fires, aiming for the body rather than the head, admonishing "No!" just as the water hits him. Drenching the dog is neither desirable nor necessary for this approach to be effective; the startle response and your disapproval are the keys. Keep in mind, I am discussing a confirmed fence fighter here, one who might try to rip an ear from another boarder's head or be injured himself, not a fence player, or a dog who occasionally and briefly tells his neighbor to take a hike. In any case, avoid the technique if winter is in full roar, and consider caging the offender.

Problem: A dog who seemed fine upon arrival becomes gradually more nervous until he seems frantic. The animal salivates to the point of foaming, regurgitates and is beset by attacks of bloody diarrhea.

Solution: Contact the client's veterinarian immediately. If the doctor is unavailable, contact your vet. In either case, let the doctor call the shots.

Problem: Soon after a dog's arrival he begins to cry and generally carry on, even to the point of howling. You recognize from the animal's aspect and timbre that he is not manifesting any sort of "bad actor" syndrome; he is lonely, and perhaps a bit frightened.

Solution: Spend a little time with the pooch. Pet him, talk with the animal, but keep your visit welcoming and brief, not consoling or prolonged. Protracted reassurance will only perpetuate the problem. Some things only the dogs themselves can sort out.

Problem: A client arrives to board a dog who appears ill. The customer assures you that the animal is just nervous, but your gut tells you the animal is sick. Now what?

Solution: Do not let the dog into your kennel, or even onto your grounds. Admittedly, this is a touchy situation: You have reserved space to board the dog, the owner is itching to leave for vacation and you are not a DVM but there is a bell sounding in the back of your mind, one that you have learned to respect, and it is telling you, "Look out!" Tell the client that you feel the animal is infirm and that you cannot board a dog whom you sense is sick. Offer to let the owner use your phone to see about having his or her veterinarian examine the pooch, but unless a vet in whom you have faith tells you that the dog is healthy, protect your other boarders.

Problem: A client who made a reservation last month arrives to board his pet, but it is obvious that the animal is in season. You have a policy of not accepting bitches in estrus. What do you do?

Solution: Reconcile yourself to the fact that you may lose this individual's business for all time when you tell him or her that you do not take females in heat. You can offer to call other kennels and the vets to try and find her a place, but putting a female in season around males can lead to a multiplicity of major problems. If you have a policy against boarding bitches in season, stick by your guns.

Problem: "Good heavens! That dog is standing outside in the rain in his run there. I wonder if I should bring him in and close his run access door?"

Solution: During an electrical storm or a freezing drizzle, yes, you should do just that. Otherwise, let the animal do as he prefers.

Rain water is not only cleansing, it's cooling. If a dog who could escape rain by stepping inside chooses to stand in it, let him. He is obviously doing what he wants to do, and—other than getting a bit soggy—he is not hurting anything.

Problem: It is time to shut down the kennel for the night, and a boarder—often a first-timer—refuses to come inside.

Solution: Try dropping a dog biscuit on the floor of his inside run, closing the run access door behind him as he enters to investigate; or, open the inside-run gate, eliminating the illusion some dogs seem to sense that the chain-link gate is closer than it actually is and appears to bar entry, and step inside the run and call pooch; or, grab a leash and go get the animal, gently.

Problem: A client wants to visit his or her pet during the several weeks the animal is scheduled to be with you (this can happen when an owner is moving, building a new house and living in temporary quarters and so on).

Solution: Though I will not accede to this type of request with a dog I am training, my attitude with boarders is "Why not?" Take the dog out of the kennel area for such visits, so not to upset the other animals. The dog should remain on your property, however. Taking the animal for a drive or a long walk can result in a troubled pooch when he is returned to the kennel. Incidentally, note the dates and times of all visits on your boarding record.

Problem: Even after reading several books on the subject, you still feel uncomfortable about canine first-aid and emergency procedures.

Solution: Veterinarians sometimes offer classes in emergency medical care for animals. Should such a course be available in your area, enroll. If such studies are not offered, meet with your vet and see if he or she would be willing to offer such a class, or to teach you privately what you need to know.

Problem: A caller wanting to make a reservation advises you that his or her pet is just getting over Parvo (or Distemper, Corona, Kennel Cough or whatever—any highly contagious disease), "But my vet says that it is alright for him to be around other dogs now."

Solution: Ask the individual to have the veterinarian call you and to tell the doctor that it is alright to answer any and all of your questions. If the caller refuses, turn down the reservation. If the caller complies (as most will), talk with the DVM when he or she calls, then contact your veterinarian. Relay the facts as you understand them and ask how risky the situation is. If there is any risk at all, do not accept the reservation.

An acquaintance once commented that she thought such a cautious attitude was too conservative; that I play it too close to the vest. Perhaps I do, but as I asked her, "Have you ever seen how quickly Parvovirus can spread? And, do you know what the mortality rate is from the disease?"

Problem: You open up the kennel one fine morning and discover that the chubby little pooch that arrived yesterday for boarding is now a skinny little pooch and the proud mother of several puppies. The owner gave you no clue the animal had been bred.

Solution: Except in exigent circumstances, get the owner's veterinarian on the phone (or call yours, if the owner's vet is unavailable), apprise him or her of the situation and arrange for the doctor to examine the dam and her offspring at your kennel as soon as possible. Do not take the dam and her pups to the vet's office; have the vet come to you: The risk of disease transmission (or injury) to the dam or her pups is just too great. The kennel call will run up the owner's vet bill, and if you're an experienced breeder you may feel that you can handle the situation without assistance, but the purpose of involving a vet is to cover yourself legally. In a courtroom, a lawyer can easily make it appear that a breeder of, say, Great Danes is not qualified to deal with the whelping of and caring for Lhasa Apso puppies or their mother.

By the way, though it may seem appropriate to confront the owner for not warning you, bear in mind that it could well be that he or she was unaware that the pooch was carrying a litter. Meaning no unkindness (or not too much at least), some owners do well to remember their pet's name.

Also, do not charge the owner extra for your time. He or she will have enough of a vet bill as it is.

Problem: Someone wishes to board a pregnant female.

Solution: I won't do it, even if she isn't scheduled to whelp for weeks and the owner is only going to be away for a few days. Simply put, there's just too much that can go wrong.

Problem: You are asked to board a dog for the mandated rabies-quarantine period after the animal bit an individual.

Solution: I will not do it. My attitude is, "Let me get this straight: You want me to accept into my kennel a dog who may have rabies? You have got to be kidding!"

Problem: Your phone rings. The caller hails from wherever and wants to board his or her pooch with you for a few days while he visits with local friends.

Solution: There is no easy, cut-and-dried answer to this one. Consider a few variables. First, you may have no way of verifying that the animal is currently vaccinated against Parvo, Distemper, Rabies and other infectious diseases. If the individual can produce a pre-printed health certificate signed by a DVM, everything is probably on the up and up (regarding vaccinations, at least). However, many travelers who take pooch along on a trip carry a vaccination record that they have maintained themselves. It may be that the notations appear on a form provided by a veterinary clinic, but lacking a vet's signature such a record is worthless in terms of authenticity. Even a signed paper can lead you to wondering if a veterinarian indeed signed the form.

Another point to consider is that for all you know the dog is currently recovering not just from an illness but from a highly contagious one. Some canine maladies can spread like wildfire, and—while the animal is *probably* healthy—do you feel comfortable in taking that chance?

Consider, too, in addition to the risks I have mentioned (and there are others; I have just touched on some of the main ones), there is a positive element to boarding any new dog that is missing in the out-of-towner instance: the opportunity to add a client to your following. In all likelihood you will never see this dog or the owner again (which you might keep in mind should you accept an out-of-town dog for boarding and find that the owner wants to pay by check). When that factor is added to the equation, I personally am even less inclined to board an out-of-town dog. The best I can do is make a few dollars, but at what risk? In sum, the safer course is to turn down the business.

Of course, there is no need to hurt someone's feelings or to make an owner angry. Rather than enumerate for the caller all the reasons why you do not take out-of-town dogs, merely advise them that your kennel is full. Lying is never "right," I agree, but it is sometimes kinder.

If you ever do take a dog from another city, here are four tips: First, get the cash in advance; second, *cash* is not a synonym for *check*; third, house the animal as far from other boarders as possible; fourth, in all other respects, treat the animal like any other, not allowing any residual misgivings to cause you to ostracize the dog.

Problem: You have contracted a remarkable case of flu—complete with fever, cramps, nausea, diarrhea, the lot—and you do not have a kennel helper.

Solution: Feel really sorry for yourself for about ten minutes, then go take care of your boarders. Today is not the day to perform a major cleaning or to repaint the building, but you must complete the basics: feeding, fresh water, clean runs. If you are a trainer, skip today's workouts. A trainer who works dogs when he or she is tired or ill seldom accomplishes much in the way of positive results.

Problem: A boarded dog just bit you, drawing blood.

Solution: Contact an MD and do as he or she tells you. If the wound is serious, respond as you would to a critical household accident: Get to a hospital emergency room or clinic, or call an ambulance. In the matter of reporting the bite to authorities, be guided by local regulations.

Problem: The following depicts a most unlikely occurrence, especially at a boarding kennel—which is why I've saved it until last—but prudence dictates that it be included: An armed individual, or one whose size is clearly more than you can safely handle, attempts to rob you.

Solution: Let him or her succeed. Remain calm. Offer no resistance whatsoever. I would even offer to carry the cash to the thief's vehicle. Don't ever fight for money. It can be replaced; you can't. If possible, occupy your mind by noting the creep's physical description and clothing. Doing so may be helpful to the police, and it may keep your fear at bay to a degree. Get a vehicle license number if you can do so safely, and note the robber's direction of departure. Once the perpetrator leaves, call the cops. Then sit down, gives thanks that you were not injured, and write down every detail you can recall about the incident, including what each of you said, and give a copy to the police when they arrive.

What if the intruder threatens to harm or steal any of the dogs? I cannot tell you what to do. I don't have that right. The smart thing, of course, is to realize that it is sometimes an irrational world, and that some situations are beyond your control. Personally, however—and I speak here *only of myself;* I do not mean to imply what course of action, if any, you should take—my thought is that if the person would harm a helpless animal, that could be a signal that I may be next. In any case, while a felon can have my money, he would have to go through me to get at a dog. Smart? No. Stupid? Probably. Inevitable? Bet on it.

Summary

This chapter has not addressed every conceivable problem that can occur when running a boarding kennel. That would not be just a book in itself, it would be a library, and even so it would be incomplete. There are simply too many variables to cover every base. Because many types of problems are similar in nature to others, though, I hope that this chapter has provided you with sufficient what-to-do-when examples to help you develop an attuned mind-set for coping effectively with difficulties that sometimes take place when boarding man's best buddy.

Reflection

Problem: After a day of dealing with two fence fighters, a feces eater who also urinates in his water bucket, a plugged-up septic line, two cancellations for what was going to be a booked-up weekend and a fear biter whose lunge caused you to whack your head on a run top as you jumped away, an old dog who has been with you many times licks your hand as you give him his evening meal. Your eyes meet; he wags his tail. You pet the animal as he tiredly leans against you. As the day sweetens beyond measure, the chronic howler in the next run seems miles away.

Solution: Enjoy the moment.

Joel McMains

10

Lessons from the Best Teacher

THE CLOSING CHAPTER of each of my training books presents anecdotes intended to teach and illuminate. That theme is also appropriate to and is continued in *Kennels and Kenneling*.

Guilty as Charged? Or Prejudged?

I was in the storeroom when the Labrador spilled his water bucket for the third time in as many hours. I heard the bucket fall and thought out loud, "This is getting just a wee bit old." The dog had been boarded with me several times before, and I had long since accepted the fact that he had a mischievous streak. He was in no way a wicked or bad-tempered dog, but more of an imp. Many times when I came upon the animal shredding a blanket, spilling food or knocking over a water bucket, his playful countenance conveyed, "Gotcha again, didn't I!"

Anyway, this particular morning found me fighting a sinus headache that was pounding out the anvil chorus, and I confess that I went to the Lab's run harboring impure, less-than-professional thoughts. But when I arrived I saw that something was different. The dog's tail was down and so was he, emotionally; I saw nervousness, anxiety and a dab of fear. Momentarily perplexed at this unexpected state, I then saw something else: the remains of a somewhat disassembled hornet on the floor near the overturned bucket.

I entered the Labrador's run, brushed what was left of the deceased bug into the clean-out trough and examined the dog for signs of having been stung, breathing a sigh of relief when I found none. I stayed with him for a time, though, in the event I had overlooked something: Dogs have been known to die from a hornet's bite. As I passed the minutes petting the animal, I took pleasure from two sources. First, the Lab gradually returned to his happy, bounce-around-the-place self. Second, I had just received a good object lesson to pass along in this book.

The spilled bucket was an accident at worst, likely related to attempts at self-defense. But even if there had been no other evidence, no gone-to-God bug, could it not have been that the bucket was accidentally toppled as the dog tried to avoid the winged intruder? Any number of explanations are possible. Moral: Don't ever have words with a dog over something that you did not see happen. To do so could be as harmful in terms of bruised spirit as a hornet sting could be in terms of physical well-being.

"Whoops!"

The Rottweiler's name was Hummel. Mine was almost mud the day the two of us reached an understanding.

Normally I will not board a dog I cannot physically handle safely in the event that I should have to contend with him. As the owner was a dear friend, in Hummel's case I made an exception. This Rotty was aggressive by nature and disinclined to obey anyone other than the gentle lady who owned him, but I felt I could get through the few days that Hummel would be with me so long as I had no physical contact with him.

Mine is a relatively quiet kennel. As a rule, the occasional yodeler soon begins to emulate the relative silence of boarders that have been here many times before. No, I do not become concerned should a dog woof at a neighbor for a bit. That's merely an expression of playfulness and as such is good exercise, but I will not abide a two-in-the-morning howler.

As I happened to walk by the outside section of Hummel's run he yelled at me. "Hush, now," I told him. With that he hit the chain-link fencing, stood on his rear legs and barked in my face, saying—or at least *I* heard him say—"In your ear!" Whether a dog is here for boarding or training, disrespect is one attitude I will not indulge. In a flash I had yanked open the run door, leapt inside, grabbed the Rotty two-handed by the skin under his jaw and began a speech that opens with "Now, you see here!" That was when I remembered just who it was that I had hold of.

Fortunately, I was able to bring it off. Once committed I stuck to my course and convinced the animal that I did not want him to give any other boarders ideas. Starting that day, Hummel's attitude toward me gradually underwent a change and we eventually became buddies. In retrospect, going beak to beak with the Rotty was perhaps not the brightest thing I have ever done, but in truth I would do it again. Knowing Rottweilers generally and this animal specifically, acceptance of his "You're lucky this fence is between us" message would have reinforced his hostile attitude, making subsequent dealings with him even more dangerous.

Now, am I saying that you yourself should physically confront the next high-powered woofer you board? Of course not. Not only is that not my message, know that more often than not I follow the course of *deflection*, which is momentarily overlooking low-risk contention or a peripheral aspect of undesirable behavior in order to prevent either from escalating. What I am telling you is twofold: First, as a boarding kennel operator, you always have to know the dog and yourself, his abilities and your limitations; and second, there may be times when you have to be an actor. Someday you may have no choice but to confront a pooch who is on the fight—the animal may make the decision for you—and a main determinant of the outcome may very well be the attitude you project. Remember, a dog who does not expect to be confronted is often taken aback when a person does respond with forceful confidence. If you radiate uncertainty, the dog may feel your hesitancy and sense that he has already won. Doubt in your mind removes doubt from his.

How Do They Know?

This one could have been titled "How Many Times I've Seen It Happen!" The following composite account stars a female German Shepherd Dog named Miranda.

One Tuesday afternoon around four o'clock she started acting antsy, trotting back and forth in her run, barking sporadically at nothing in particular. I commented to my kennel helper that Mike—Miranda's owner—would probably be picking up the dog soon.

"But Miranda's not scheduled to go out for a couple of days yet. Did he call and say that he'd be along this afternoon?"

"Nope. Haven't heard a word from him, but I expect he'll be here within a couple of hours."

"What makes you think so?" my apprentice asked.

"Just look at how Miranda's acting. She senses he's coming," I replied.

"Joel, give me a break. So the animal is more active than usual. That doesn't mean anything."

"Maybe not, but a pizza says Mike will be here before six."

"You're on!"

Mike arrived a little after five and collected Miranda, my kennel helper dithered about and muttered to herself for awhile and I soon observed the truism that pizza tastes best when someone else pays for it.

How do they know? I have no earthly notion, but I know they often do. I have witnessed the phenomenon too many times to ignore it. An hour or two prior to an owner's unscheduled arrival, some dogs, usually those who are well bonded to their people, become active. They sniff the air, bark, stare toward the driveway and communicate a sense of anticipation. Would I call the attribute spooky? No; mysterious perhaps, but not eerie. It is simply another canine ability.

Look Out, Expert!

Though you may not be a breeder or a trainer, the public may perceive you as being knowledgeable in both areas of dog keeping. Occasionally you may be asked to evaluate a dog. Though your first impulse may be one of service and helpfulness—and of promoting your kennel—be careful. Be very, very careful.

The Doberman appeared friendly enough as he leash-pulled his owner to my gate. The man had called earlier, asking if I would help him find a home for the dog. I receive many such calls, as well as contacts from people looking to acquire a pet, and my practice is to take the person's name and phone number, and post them and other information (breed, gender, age and so forth) on my bulletin board in hopes that I will hear of a match. Something in this caller's tone caught my attention, however, and though it is not my usual practice, I asked that he bring his dog by for a once-over.

A few minutes of discussion with the owner found me on one knee in front of and slightly to the dog's right. I was caressing the back of the Dobe's neck with my left hand, and my right hand was near the left center of the animal's chest. The dog was enjoying the contact, all was well. Then, all at once the Dobe went rigid, his pupils expanded and he attacked me. I don't mean he nipped in my direction—he exploded: full-mouth lunges and intense growling.

I learned a long time ago that the safest course when beset by a nearby canine is to move no more than is absolutely necessary. Get what anatomy you must out of harm's way, yes, but use as little movement to do so as possible. The reason for this is akin to the notion of not running when near a swarm of bees or hornets: Swift motion can excite and attract the insects. My reflexes took over—there was no time for conscious thought—and it happened that I was spared injury.

To this day, though, I can mentally replay the incident in slow motion with vivid detail and clarity. The Doberman's first assault was toward my face. I pulled my head back just enough that he lost interest and redirected his focus toward the faster motion of my left hand, which I was rapidly moving up and away from the dog, knowing at a subliminal level that doing so would make it his next target, and that he would not be able to reach it.

How close was it? I felt the dog's breath on my face, and his whiskers on my cheek as he changed direction toward my hand, and then his muzzle hair on the palm of my raised left hand as the leash tightened and prevented any further advance. At no time did I stand; that takes too long, and had I done so the animal likely would have reacted by taking me in the leg. How long did the event last? Maybe three seconds, certainly no more than that. Did I see the attack coming? Yes, but only a blink before it began. Nothing in the dog's aspect had even hinted at hostility before then.

My purpose in relating this tale is to point out two dangers inherent in dealing closely with unknown canines. The first is obvious: Dogs can unjustly and without provocation launch an all-out war within a millisecond. They have the ability to go from relative dormancy to full-on and flat-out in less than a heartbeat. The second risk is less obvious: In such a situation, don't expect any help from the owner. You may have noticed that I did not tell you that the man "hurriedly pulled his dog back." That's because he didn't. My full attention was on the Doberman, you understand, but I was aware that the owner did not move a muscle; he just stood there with his mouth hanging open, watching the show. Nor did the leash holder advise me ahead of time that the dog had—without apparent cause—previously attacked several people in similar fashion, though it developed that the animal had done just exactly that. Nice of the guy to warn me, don't you think?

Is this tale a typical event in my daily living? No, thank God. Such events are extremely rare. So why have I told you about such an admittedly isolated incident? Because you work with dogs, because you need to know what can happen and because in such circumstances, rare though they be, all it may take is once to cause you serious injury. Better you should learn the need for caution from these pages than from an emergency-room visit. As I told you in the opening paragraph, when dealing with dogs you do not know, especially with breeds new to your experience, "Be very, very careful."

"Can You Believe It?"

This one didn't directly involve me, but a veterinary clinic/boarding kennel in another state. The account presents an object lesson in how not to run a boarding operation.

The owners of a large dog boarded at the facility sent a friend to pick up the animal so that she—the dog—would be at home when their flight arrived later that evening. Mistake number one: The clinic released the dog to a total stranger, relying only on the man's word.

Friend drove pooch to the owner's ranch, and upon opening his vehicle's door was unable to prevent the dog from bolting. Mistake number two: The clinic had neglected to return the owner's leash. Then the real tragedy occurred.

The dog saw some horses nearby and began to chase them along and into barbed-wire fencing. The horses' panic quickly spread to the man, who grabbed a rifle from his pickup and, lacking any safer option, killed the dog. When the owners arrived hours later, mistake number three was discovered. That's right: The kennel had given the friend the wrong dog.

The owner's dog was still in a run at the clinic. She was of the same breed and gender as the now cooling carcass in the owner's corral, and because their friend had never seen their dog before, he had no way of realizing the error as it was being made.

Now, if this hasn't been enough to raise your blood pressure, perhaps the postscript will do it. The owners contacted the clinic and reclaimed their dog, the clinic called the owner of the deceased animal who, it happened, had never seen a horse in her life and the clinic's predominant reaction was to grouse about both owners' refusal to pay their bills.

As I said: How not to run a boarding facility.

A "Cost" of Doing Business

Operating a boarding kennel can bring great enjoyment. As I once commented to a friend, "It is hard to believe that people are willing to pay me good money to do what I like doing: spending time with dogs." But, as with any endeavor, there is a darker side, a price, one might say. Consider the following example.

Your phone rings. Calling is a client of long standing. You think to yourself, "How nice! Mugsy is going to come visit me for a time." You ask, "So, what can I do for you today, Fred?"

"That's why I'm calling. We had to put Mugsy to sleep last week. Just got too old. I knew that you'd want to know; you and her were always such buddies and all."

So you spend some time talking with Fred, saying whatever you can to offer comfort. After awhile you both say good-bye, you hang up the phone and you hope that it won't ring again for awhile.

To be sure, Mugsy's passing is much tougher on Fred and his family than it is on you. They raised the animal from a pup; she was part of their family for many years; your contact with her was relatively infrequent. Their house will be hushed for a time; yours will be back to normal much sooner. But even though Mugsy's death doesn't even begin to upset you like it does the owner, it does mist the eyes; the day is less bright than it was moments before. Moreover—and this is the price I mentioned earlier—it won't happen to you once, but many, many times. The owner struggles with one big impact. You endure many little ones.

Some People . . .

In chapter 4, "Startup," I advise against having too complicated or exacting a rate structure. Consider the case of an outfit that had excellent facilities and good personnel, but one that nearly sank itself under the weight of its own rate plan.

The day the kennel opened its doors it had five different rates, which were based on breed of dog. A most impressive chart graced the office wall, grouping the various breeds under separate rate headings. All very neat and methodical. The kennel owner had but to look at the boarder, glance at the chart and assign a rate. Perhaps you've guessed the oversight. Sure, it wasn't long until someone showed up to board a Heinz-57, and no one knew quite what to do.

So the kennel altered its policy to one of charging according to each dog's weight, which is fine for as far as the concept goes, but these people took it to extremes, weighing every dog they boarded, like so much hamburger. Further, the kennel owner decreed a policy that if a dog was even an ounce or two into the next category, "We charge accordingly." A kennel helper asked, "What about when we someday board a dog who is several years old, has gained a pound or two since we saw him last, but who has been a steady boarder with us since he was a pup? Hiking the rate in a case like that is asking for resentment from clients, isn't it?" The man didn't bat an eye as he reaffirmed, "We charge accordingly."

Finally things came full circle. One day a customer showed up with a large dog who was fractionally into the next category. The client pointed out that the weight of the dog's collar was enough to make the difference. The owner replied that the collar was part of the dog; the client said, "C'mon Barnaby. Let's get out of this joint and go someplace where they care about *you* as much as they do fitting square pegs into square holes." That night the kennel owner called a friend of mine who was also in the business, and asked for some guidance: "What am I doing wrong?"

As my friend later told me, "He's a nice enough duck, Joel, but he's got no feel for dealing with people. Great facilities, a good location, very well organized, likes dogs, but when it comes to getting along with his fellow man, zero." Exactly what my friend told the gentleman I do not know, but I can make a good guess. It was probably pretty similar to what you or I might suggest: There is nothing wrong with a rate structure based on boarders' weights, but plunking pooch onto a scale bespeaks too rigid an attitude—an experienced dog person should be able to eyeball a dog and determine the animal's weight with sufficient exactitude to assign a rate—and when the result is iffy, give the client a break. "Well, pup, you're a shade into the next category, but what's a few ounces between friends?" Whenever possible, whether the subject is kennel design, quality of equipment or customer relations, take the long-term view. Those who don't can end up with memories of a short-term business.

When Push Doth Come to Shove

I mentioned in chapter 7, "Policies, Practices and Direction," some approaches to try with your food supplier to lower your dog-food cost. Years ago a kennel operator friend of mine found that his supplier turned a deaf ear to any requests for a price break. My friend was on the verge of switching to another food, which he didn't want to do, when an idea came to him. He advised the supplier that he—the kennel operator—would not only tell his boarding clients that he was using another (nationally recognized, very good) brand of food, but he would also tell them that he would not feed "that slop (referring to the brand of food that he was actually using) to a junkyard dog." The supplier relented.

I am fortunate that my food supplier is a longtime friend, and that the need for such gamesmanship has never existed. However, I also recognize that one has to look after one's own interests first, and on that basis I have to admire my kennel operator friend's adroit use of *chutzpa*.

The Art of Compromise

Tiny was a male Rottweiler. I'm not saying that the three-year-old was exceptionally large, but each of his front paws was the approximate size of Ohio. He was a bright, good-natured animal who spent a month with me some years ago learning the basics of companion obedience.

After Tiny's owner went off I escorted the animal to his run (in truth, the dog more or less dragged me to the area where he could hear other dogs, but that's another story). After removing his leash and collar, I spent a few minutes with the dog, getting to know him, and then took my leave. As you know from chapter 6, "Comings and Goings," I habitually put new arrivals in their outside runs, momentarily keeping the door to the inside run closed to allow the animals to learn that some things are better done outdoors than indoors. I followed this practice with Tiny, and after removing his collar and petting the animal for a bit, I left, put a leash on a Pomeranian who was also here for obedience training and proceeded to the training yard.

As Tiny's run was visible from the training area, I glanced in his direction from time to time to see how he was getting along. I noticed that he seemed particularly intrigued with the metal sliding door leading to the indoor area, but that he otherwise seemed to be adapting well to his new environment. Then, several minutes later, just as the Pom and I were finishing our training session and were walking back to the kennel, I observed that Tiny was near the end of his run farthest from the building, and that he was pawing the concrete while staring toward the metal run-access door. His head was slightly down, his butt was up, his concentration was absolute and about the time I asked myself, "What in the world?" the answer dawned in "Oh, Lord!" fashion as the animal flew in full Rotty gallop-hop toward the door. As he struck the object with commendable force I hurriedly told the Pom what fine work she had done that morning, put her in her run and raced into the building.

It came as no surprise that Tiny was uninjured—I think that he could have rammed a tank without hurting himself—but the door was finished. Dangling from its overhead-pulley chain, the object was bowed inward as though a stick of dynamite had been ignited next to it. One of the tracks in which the door used to slide had been torn from the wall. Seeing this, I reacted in my usual calm, unruffled, professional manner: "What the hell do you think you are trying to do?"

To this day I can still see Tiny's expression—confident, proud and radiating a message of accomplishment: "Trying? What do you mean, 'trying'? I've done it. When's lunch?" His abbreviated tail was fluttering, the animal was obviously quite pleased with himself and I decided that the best solution was to reach a compromise: I would not reattach the door if he would agree not to knock it off again.

Moral: Some problems are better deflected than confronted. Given the warm weather and the fact that the dog would likely not encounter such a door at his home, I removed what was left of the object and decided not to push the issue. In truth, the Rotty was unaware that he had done anything "wrong"; moreover, he was proud of his "achievement." I could have taken the animal to task over the incident, but not only would that have taught him nothing positive, doing so could have easily cast a negative pall over his arrival here. Given that he was an emotionally sensitive dog, as many Rottweilers are, I reasoned that it was better to sluff off the event than to make it a focal point. As it turned out, Tiny manifested no other destructive tendencies, he was as trainable as he was large and I attached a new door a few hours after he went home four weeks later.

A One-Person Anti-Brutality League

Like the section entitled "Can You Believe It?" this one did not happen to me. It took place at the kennel of a friend whom I was visiting and I have her permission to relate it to you.

The Siberian Husky had been boarded at my friend's kennel for a little over three weeks. The day the dog's owner arrived to get the pooch, I watched my boarding kennel friend almost wind up with a battle on her hands—not with the dog, with the owner.

My friend asked the man to wait several yards from the kennel

186

while she went to leash up the dog. As she was returning with the Siberian in tow, the owner hollered to her, "Cut him loose." So my friend dropped the leash and the excited animal scampered to the owner. Just as the dog neared him, the owner yelled at the Husky to "Sit, Sit, Sit, Sit." I knew from being around the animal that he had no obedience training, but owners sometimes feel that their pets should be mind readers. The dog did not sit, of course, but jumped happily on the owner. That was when the man struck the dog in the head with a fist and my friend lost her cool.

I won't detail my friend's exact choice of words—they would never get past my editor, anyway—but her message essentially pointed out that the owner had said to release an obviously excited dog, one that clearly did not know from obedience but was overjoyed at seeing his owner—"But I will never know why!"—and that the owner's brutal response to getting what he asked for was totally out of line and would not be tolerated at my friend's kennel. It was really quite something to witness. The owner was well over six feet, and my friend was about five-foot-nothing; nonetheless, she backed the owner up several steps as she laid down the law.

Yes, in the boarding kennel business—like any other—one sometimes has to play certain games; on occasion you have to tacitly accept minor irritants in order to keep customers coming back. But when some dodo takes a hot-tempered action that could injure a dog, my friend sees her obligation much like I do: to protect the dog, and if that leads the owner to go elsewhere in the future, so be it. Such happenings are extremely rare, of course, but they can occur, and better you should realize that sad fact now. It is a part of the business.

Incidentally, the owner later took his dog through my obedience classes. Both learned a great deal about the other, and to my knowledge there has never been a repetition of the slug-the-dog incident.

A Case of the Sads

Of the many dogs I've had the pleasure of training, Puppy was in the top five in terms of trainability. The male Labrador was with me for four weeks of companion obedience, and was subsequently boarded at my kennel several times. It was during one of the times he was boarded that the trouble developed.

Part of the problem's origin was timing. During one occasion when the dog was boarded with me for a week, his owner collected the animal and then—because of an unforeseen situation—had to bring him back for further boarding less than twenty-four hours later. As I put Puppy in his run his spirit drooped; it was too much too soon. The fact that there were several dogs here for training did not help his morale; he came to see that they got leash time but that he did not. In the space of a couple of hours, Puppy became as depressed as any dog I have ever seen.

Now, as we both know, some dogs are manipulative: They will manifest ''the pitifulness of myself'' syndrome for the attention it usually brings them. That does not make them bad dogs; generally, it is what they have learned is necessary. But Puppy was as guileless a dog as you would ever meet. Subterfuge was just not part of his nature.

So the question becomes one of what to do. Various medications are available for bodily ills, but what of maladies of the spirit? One boarding kennel acquaintance opined that it was not worth worrying about, that ''There's enough to do without fretting over a boarder's state of mind.'' She was wrong, of course, as emotional well-being can directly affect physical health. Besides, Puppy was special. He had gotten under my skin a long time ago. A part of the boarding kennel profession is the fact that you will be attracted more to some dogs than to others. Anyone who denies that truth either has an emotional hide like a rhino or has not been in the business very long. Still, how to give Puppy that push that would allow him to bring himself back up?

The answer was simple: I added him to my training string. Sure, he already knew the work—quite well, in fact—but the few minutes a couple of times daily that I worked him lent purpose to this visit; he found that he was here for a reason. His owner had not found him displeasing shortly after pickup. There is no way to know, of course, but I suspect that feelings akin to that were what was bothering the dog.

You may not be a trainer or even have any interest in the field, but should an animal you know to normally be outgoing and full of life arrive and display an attitude lower than a snake's arch, the simple act of taking him for a brief on-leash walk can make all the difference. Don't just cut him loose in an exercise yard—that won't do it—spend some time with the pooch, marveling at what a truly fine animal he is, petting him. Your efforts will be well rewarded.

Incidentally, if you are wondering if I charged Puppy's owner additionally for the extra time spent with the dog, the answer is no, I did not. The problem was mine (and Puppy's), not the owner's, and no brush-up training time had been requested. Would I do the same thing—spend extra but unpaid time with a dog who needs it—even with a dog who is not "special"? Of course. Wouldn't you?

I Wish I'd Known

If you plan to erect a concrete-block kennel, there is an oddity about concrete-block fabrication that is well worth knowing: Though they appear uniform, not all blocks are precisely the same size. This is no problem when the length or height of a block is, say, a sixteenth of an inch longer or shorter than another; one can compensate for the imprecision by adjusting the amount of mortar used to join the block to one next to it. The problem that can be unforeseen concerns blocks that are too deep. Since those sides are not mortared, the excess depth has to appear either inside or outside the building; that is, the choice is whether the outside or the inside of a wall will have an occasional slight protrusion of block.

Masons tend to build so that the excess of a too-wide block is placed to the inside of the wall, not the outside. They do this out of custom, being used to the fact that a carpenter can adjust the slight bulge during the interior framing. However, make sure that any such imperfections are placed to the *outside* of the building, not to the inside. If this is not done, and if you elect to install vertically sliding run-access doors, you may find that some doors open stiffly and do not close at all. Why? Because if in opening they slide over a protruding block, gravity exerts insufficient attraction to free the door from the protrusion. In that situation one discovers the joys of removing the door unit from the wall, grinding down the too-deep block(s) to acceptable tolerances, repainting the affected area—which necessitates keeping the dogs outside while the paint dries—and rehanging the door.

How do I know about this problem? Don't ask!

The Need to Commune

Lupis was a two-year-old wolf hybrid. He was easy to get along with, took well to being boarded and was generally easygoing and friendly, if somewhat independent, which is typical of that type of animal. He had a habit, though, that is well worth pondering.

Every night, as I'd begin to shut down the kennel, he walked outside, stood in his run, laid his head back and bayed for a few minutes. Then he entered his inside run, received his nightly dog biscuit and settled for the night.

I've mentioned that mine is a quiet kennel, which is how I like it. Earlier in this chapter, I pointed out that "I will not abide a two-in-the-morning howler." But Lupis wasn't in that category. He was not trying to be a pest or a nuisance; he was merely going through his nighttime/sleeptime ritual. We could debate motivation all day long, but my sense was that the animal was doing something that he needed to do in order to rest, saying good night to that which guides him, much as a child might say his prayers.

Moral: Regardless of your kennel's rules and practices, always remember the natures of what you're boarding; never forbid a dog to be a dog.

That's It, for Now

The "Lessons from the Best Teacher" chapter is always among my favorites to write as it allows me a stroll down memory lane, gifting me a chuckle here and a shake of the head there. I hope you have enjoyed reading this one and that you have profited from its content.

Reflection

The dogs eat of the crumbs which fall from their masters' table.
Matt. 15:27

Postscript

An ACQUAINTANCE ONCE ASKED, "With your computer expertise, why do you stay in this nutty business? The hours are long, the work is often hard and demanding and there's certainly no money in it." I shrugged, and muttered, "It's what I do, I guess," knowing the answer to be beyond the individual's comprehension.

But the truth is that when a dog is brought to me for training, very often the animal is nearly out of control, frantic. Straining at the leash, unmindful of his owner's presence, the pooch seems driven to run, to search.

Later, when starting the dog's training, I first acquaint him with the fact of my existence. Within seconds the animal suddenly freezes in place. He settles. A peace beyond mere relaxation warms over him and as we lock eyes it's as though he says, "Oh—there you are. I've been looking for you." Of course, it is not an individual the animal has been seeking, but a leader, an Alpha.

I have to agree that wealth may never result from canine contact, but richness does. How it surely does!

Canine First Aid

I do not claim to be a veterinarian. The following reference chart is a compendium of several similar works and of my own experience. It is intended solely for emergency situations when your vet can't be reached and it is offered with this caveat: If at all possible, contact a vet before treating any condition!

Problem	Symptoms	Treatments
ANAL GLANDS	The scoots, excessive rectal licking, bloody abscess discharge	Have a vet clear glands; be watchful for ruptured abscess; check for tapeworms.
ANIMAL BITES	Skin tears, swelling, drainage	Clip hair around wounds, wash with soap and water, do not bandage, allow to drain; take to vet if deep or needs stitches.
BLEEDING FROM CUTS	*Artery*: Uneven flow, bright red blood *Vein*: Steady flow, dark red blood	*Artery*: Apply tourniquet between wound and heart. *Vein*: Apply tourniquet on side of wound away from heart.

Problem	Symptoms	Treatments
BLEEDING FROM CUTS		Use pressure bandage if tourniquet not possible; release pressure at 15- to 20-minute intervals.

NOTE: Tourniquets are required only for life-threatening lacerations of large vessels (i.e., femoral or radial arteries). For most hemorrhage situations, using firm, direct pressure over the wound for 10 to 15 minutes is adequate to control bleeding. Additionally, improperly applied tourniquets can lead to severe tissue damage or even to loss of a limb or a digit.

Problem	Symptoms	Treatments
BLEEDING INTERNAL	Weakness, gums pale gray or white, prostration	Keep dog quiet, use a stretcher to move and do so carefully; this condition is possible even when there is no apparent injury; take to vet immediately.
BROKEN BONES, DISLOCATIONS	Inability to stand or to use legs, intense pain	Immobilize dog as best you can; use stretcher to move; use a temporary splint only on leg bones; don't try to set a bone—take dog to vet! Don't try to bandage or splint pelvis, withers (shoulders) or ribs.
BURNS—ACID	Obvious	Apply moist solution of baking soda or similar alkali.
BURNS—CAUSTIC	Obvious	Apply cold water; take dog to vet.
BURNS—FIRE OR HEAT	Obvious	If over a small area, apply a household burn remedy/pain killer.
BURNS—HOT WATER	Obvious	Douse liberally with cold water

> With any burn case, take dog to vet if more than a small area is affected.

NOTE: For all burns (chemical as well as thermal), simple application of cold water rinses is the safest and most effective initial treatment. One exception is large-area second- or third-degree burns from any cause, which should immediately be examined by a vet.

194

Problem	Symptoms	Treatments
DIARRHEA	Obvious	No food for 12 hours; if sure a toxin has not been ingested, use Pepto-Bismol at 1cc per 10 pounds of body weight; add cooked rice to food; take dog to vet if persists more than 12 hours.
DROWNING	Obvious	Hold dog up by rear legs to remove water; lay on side to apply artificial respiration; keep warm when revived.
EARS	Shaking, scratching excessively, inflamed ear canal, malodorous liquid	Clean outer area of ear with alcohol and cotton; have vet examine. If ears are bloody or are inflamed, do not use alcohol (it would be too painful); take dog to a vet.
EYES	Inflammation, cuts, scratches	Wash using eye lotion or boric acid solution; use a triple-antibiotic ophthalmic ointment (one that does not contain cortisone) as a general, all-purpose treatment; don't use plain water as it may irritate eyes.
FISH HOOKS	Usually in mouth, lip or foot	Cut off barb or eye end of hook and work out very carefully; never pull the barb back through.
FLEAS and TICKS	Intense scratching and chewing	Have dog dipped at vet's; treat your premises; burn the dog's bedding; check skin weekly.
FOREIGN OBJECTS	Coughing, choking, pawing at mouth; shaking of head often indicates object is in throat; persistent vomiting can mean it is in the intestinal tract.	Examine mouth, tongue, gums, teeth; use handkerchief to hold tongue to examine throat; use fingers or tweezers to remove object; if it is deeply imbedded, take dog to vet.
HEATSTROKE	Lying prone, staring, difficulty breathing	Place in partly filled tub of cold water or douse

Problem	Symptoms	Treatments
HEATSTROKE		liberally; must quickly reduce body temperature, especially that of the brain.
HIT BY A VEHICLE	Dragging, limping, paralysis, cuts, raw or burned skin areas, grease on coat	Keep dog warm and quiet; stop bleeding; support fractures with newspaper pads; be alert for symptoms of shock; protect self, as dog may not recognize you and may attack out of fear and pain; carefully transport to veterinarian immediately.
POISONING	Retching, trembling, pain, convulsions, diarrhea, depression, weakness, staggering, dizziness, salivation, loss of appetite	Induce vomiting by giving: 1) Equal parts of water and hydrogen peroxide at 2 tbsp. per 10 pounds of body weight, or 2) 4 to 6 tsp. of salt diluted in a glass of water, or 3) mustard and water, or 4) 2 tsp. of salt on back of tongue; when stomach is empty, give egg white or milk; take dog to vet; try to determine type and amount of poison ingested.

NOTE: Vomiting should *not* be induced if caustic chemicals or petroleum products were ingested. Also, in cases where it is proper to induce vomiting, doing so is effective only within 4 to 6 hours of ingestion of poison. Last, vomiting should only be induced if the animal is conscious and alert.

Problem	Symptoms	Treatments
PORCUPINE QUILLS	Unmistakable; dog in pain	Hold dog between your legs, or have a second person hold him; then twist out quills using pliers, starting in chest area.
RUNNING FITS	Running about in wide circles; dog acts as if he is about to convulse.	When dog falls, attach a collar and leash; cover dog if possible; dog may not recognize you and may try to bite, so protect yourself; take to vet immediately.
SHOCK	Nervousness or prostration, weak pulse,	Keep dog quiet; discourage movement; keep warm;

Problem	Symptoms	Treatments
	shallow breathing, pale gums, glassy eyes	shock can accompany any injury or extreme fright; take to vet immediately.
SKUNKS	Eyes are often sprayed, causing dog to paw at them.	Wash eyes well with boric acid solution; dry dog and soak ASAP with Massengill douche or a commercial product; don't wash dog first as that makes oily scent fluid travel over a larger area; examine dog for bites and take to vet if dog has been bitten, as skunks may be rabid.
SPRAINS	Limping, swelling	Cold packs for first 12 hours. Ask a vet to recommend a specific product for pain relief.
VOMITING	Obvious	Stop all food and water for 12 hours; then give small amounts of broth (cooled), cottage cheese and bread crumbs; take to vet if condition persists longer than 12 hours.
WORMS	Weight loss, dull/dry coat, appetite change, depression, diarrhea, vomiting, visible worms	Take fresh fecal sample to vet for analysis; if positive, treat according to vet's instructions; avoid generic wormers.

EMERGENCY TELEPHONE NUMBERS

_____ _____   _____ _____
_____ _____   _____ _____
_____ _____   _____ _____
_____ _____   _____ _____
_____ _____   _____ _____

INDEX

About the Author

JOEL McMAINS has been training and boarding dogs professionally since 1976. In addition to offering contract obedience and protection training services, he holds public obedience classes and training seminars. Joel is certified by POST (Peace Officer's Standards and Training Commission) as a Police Service K-9 Trainer and Instructor for the state of Wyoming. He is retired as the Chief K-9 Trainer for the Sheridan County Sheriff's Department and for the City of Sheridan Police Department. Joel has testified in court proceedings as an expert witness, has taught a course in K-9 selection, management, training and deployment for the Police-Science Division of Sheridan College, and has been the coordinator of Sheridan County's 4-H dog program since 1982. He is the author of *Dog Logic—Companion Obedience* and *Advanced Obedience Training—Easier Than You Think!* and is a member of the Dog Writers' Association of America. Both titles are published by Howell Book House.